Faith ae

Faith and Common Sense

Faith and Common Sense

Living boldly, choosing wisely

David Dewey

Scripture Union, 207–209 Queensway, Bletchley, MK2 2EB, England.
Email: info@scriptureunion.org.uk
Internet: http://www.scriptureunion.org.uk

© Copyright David Dewey 2000
First published 2000

ISBN 1 85999 302 8

British Library Cataloguing-in-Publication Data
A catalogue record for this book is available from the British Library.

Cover design by ie Design.
Printed and bound in Great Britain by Cox & Wyman Ltd, Reading,
Berkshire.

CONTENTS

INTRODUCTION

I had taken out my cheque book and was about to hand over the deposit on a second-hand car. We had been through a series of old bangers – it was all we could afford – and this was going to be yet another one. I knew it was a false economy because none of them lasted more than a year or so and there were frequent heavy repair bills. We did not want or need a brand new car, just something a little more reliable and a little less expensive to run. We had made it a matter for prayer, but no answer seemed forthcoming.

Just as I took the cap off my pen, the phone rang. It was Sarah, my wife. She had tracked me down to the place where I was buying the car. 'Stop!' she said. 'Don't buy it! Come home! I'll explain when you get here.' What on earth, I thought, was she up to? But I trusted her enough to do as she asked. I made my excuses, closed my cheque book and left.

I arrived home to discover that, while I had been out, Christian friends had called Sarah to say they had been 'led' by the Lord to make us a financial gift – a rather generous one, as it turned out. They had no idea of our need to replace our car. With the gift I was able to buy a better car, one I had my eye on, still second-hand, but more reliable, more economical to run and less prone to breakdowns. It served us well for a number of years.

I have changed cars several times since that day sixteen years ago, and nothing like that has ever happened again. No phone calls. No surprise gifts of money. No divine interventions. Every time it has been a matter of practical common sense. What can we afford? What trade-in value might we get? How many miles to the gallon? What size do we need now the children have left home? What about insurance and servicing costs? And so on.

This is not to say that more recent purchases have been any less a matter for prayer, but direction has come through common sense rather than obvious or dramatic divine intervention. And this is what this book is about: faith and common sense. Are these contrary or complementary to one another? When should we follow the direction indicated by common sense, and when should we step out in adventurous faith?

Although we will look at the subject of guidance in the final chapter, this is not primarily what this book is about. It is, first and foremost, an exploration of the nature of faith. In Part 1 we will look at some Bible characters and uncover some Bible principles. We will find examples of bold faith (Peter walking on the water) and examples of steady faithfulness (Ruth in the Old Testament and Zechariah in the New). In looking at them, we will discover that we cannot understand the nature of faith without understanding the nature of God: how he interacts with the world he has made through both natural and supernatural means. All this is in Part 1.

In Part 2 we will examine some of those areas in life with which Christians most frequently struggle: healing, the gifts of the Spirit, the worlds of work and money, coping with failure and, finally, discovering God's guidance. At the end of each chapter in Part 2 there are suggestions for further reading together with a number of questions. These can be used for either personal reflection or group discussion. My hope and prayer is that this book will in some small way help to encourage common sense and build faith in those who read it.

> Faith is being sure of what we hope for and certain of what we do not see.
>
> *(Hebrews 11:1)*

❧ Note

Other Bible versions besides the NIV are indicated by abbreviations: Contemporary English Version (CEV); Living Bible (LB); New Living Translation (NLT); New Revised Standard Version (NRSV); Revised English Bible (REB).

PART ONE: PRINCIPLES

❧ *Chapter One* ❧

'AND PETER...'

'And Peter walked on the water.' The preacher repeated the sentence over and over. It punctuated his sermon at regular intervals. If he said it once, he must have said it fifty times. *'And-Pet-er-walked-on-the-wat-er.'* Each syllable was drawn out for maximum effect.

It took me under two minutes to decide I did not like this sermon or this preacher. It had been a mistake ever to invite him to come, to occupy *my* pulpit. This was too far removed from a sound three-point sermon: this guy had barely one point to his talk. High on rhetoric, poor on content, was my verdict. I could just imagine what would be said at the next leaders' meeting about *my* having invited him to preach.

After sitting through this for fifteen minutes, with no end in sight, I began to feel uncomfortable – but now it was for a different reason. Through this poorly constructed, near contentless sermon, God was speaking, and he was speaking to me. Would I have acted like Peter? Would I have got out of the boat? Did I have the faith to take a risk like that – in the way I led the church, in the way I prayed for people, in the way I trusted God for the future? Or was I the kind of Christian who, unless pushed, preferred to stay put as Peter's co-disciples had done? Carefully considering all my options before doing anything rash that might rock the boat, let alone get out of it. Never making a move without studiously weighing up what might go wrong and being sure I had a clear route back to safety.

The story of Simon Peter walking on the water (Matt 14:22–33) is one we often think of as 'for the Sunday School', but it speaks powerfully to us as believing adults too. Even if you are very familiar with the story, why not read it again right now? Try to read it as though for the first time. It really is quite bizarre: Jesus and then Peter walk across the storm-driven waves of Lake Galilee.

On hundreds, maybe even thousands of occasions, Peter had got into a boat. He was a fisherman, after all. Each time he pushed off from the shore, he was exercising a kind of faith: that the boat would stay afloat and keep him dry, that it would get him safely to his destination. He did this so often he probably did it without thinking. Experience and common sense told him that his boat would keep him above the waves. But this time was to be different. Peter was to discover he could stay above the waves *without the boat*.

Jesus had sent his twelve disciples across Lake Galilee, remaining behind by himself to pray. The disciples were soon in difficulty. A sudden storm had blown up and the normally calm surface of the lake was whipped into a frenzy. With the wind against them, they were barely making any headway. All through the long hours of darkness they rowed. Then, at the dead of night, sometime between three and six in the morning, they caught sight of something, or someone, off the stern. The disciples, big burly fishermen among them, turned to jelly. They thought they were seeing a ghost or some kind of apparition. What, or who, was it? A super-natural omen of impending disaster? Death?

The figure came closer still, within hailing distance. Thirty yards, now twenty. Then a voice called out, 'Take courage! It is I. Don't be afraid.' It sounded like Jesus, but they were not sure. Peter – and only Peter – replied: 'Lord, if it's you, tell me to come to you on the water.'

'Come,' said Jesus.

Without further hesitation, Peter climbed out of the boat and walked towards Jesus. All the while the storm was raging: the wind and waves did not die down until after Jesus and Peter were back in the vessel, awash with water as it was.

Peter's actions appear to lack any basis in common sense, but this is not the case. Far from lacking discern-ment, his faith was actually very perceptive. First, he already had two good reasons to be certain that Jesus had power over the forces of nature. Just a few hours previously, he and the other disciples had seen him use five small loaves and two fishes to feed a crowd of thou-sands (14:13–21). Second, Peter did not simply leap out of the boat: he waited until Jesus called him. If he had got out without being commanded to do so by the Lord, we can be sure he would have sunk like a stone.

Two things must come together before we can attempt to exercise water-walking faith. First, we must believe God has the power. Second, we must know that it is God's will for us in our particular situation. God's general will and God's specific will must come together.

Peter had faith. He believed – at least momentarily. He saw that Jesus had power over nature, and realised that if Jesus could walk on water, he could enable him to walk on water too. And Peter nearly made it. Only at the last minute did he panic, taking his eyes off Jesus to look at the weather conditions. Intriguingly, he was defeated not by the insubstantiality of the water beneath his feet, but by the strength of the wind at his back. It was not that he thought Jesus was too weak, but that the enemy was too powerful. It was not his lack of faith that let him down, but his fear of what he was up against. As he sank, he quickly cried out to Jesus – definitely the right thing to do – and was at once rescued by him. Side by side, master and disciple walked back to the boat and climbed aboard. Only then did the wind and waves calm down.

Through this incident, Peter and the other disciples learnt something about Jesus. Their response was worship and a deepening of their faith: 'You really are the Son of God' (v 33, NLT). In his account, Matthew presents Peter as both a good and a not-so-good example of faith. He is a good example in that he alone out of all twelve disciples was prepared to step out of the boat. Peter's actions were impetuous, but they were also motivated by faith. It is real faith of obedient action, not conjecture or postulation. He did not stop at theory: 'Now I know I could walk on water if so required.' He trusted, and acted upon that trust. For a brief moment at least, his faith in Jesus overcame his fear of the wind and waves. Even when he was sinking, it was to Jesus and not his colleagues in the boat that he cried out. That, too, is faith.

In another sense, however, this is a story about doubt

and the testing of God. Notice what Peter said before he climbed out of the boat: 'Lord, if it's you...' But Jesus, walking on the water, had already identified himself. Peter wanted to believe but had doubts – he was not entirely sure that it was Jesus out there and not a phantom or some malevolent spirit.

By asking Jesus to invite him to step out of the boat, Peter was revealing not just his faith but also his doubts. God was testing his faith, but he was in danger of putting God to the test, something scripture frequently warns against (Deut 6:16; Matt 4:7). This explains Jesus' apparently harsh rebuke: 'You don't have much faith. Why did you doubt me?' (NLT). Peter's water-walking efforts were more to bolster a weak faith than to prove a strong faith. But at least he got out of the boat. The other disciples remained firmly inside it. I wonder what I would have done? What would you have done?

The purpose of this book is to look at the question of faith. When, if ever, are we to exercise the kind of seemingly reckless, impulsive, spontaneous faith that Peter at least partly demonstrates – the kind of faith that goes against all logic and common sense? And when are we to exercise more cautious faith, which, while worshipping Jesus as the Son of God, nevertheless stays in the boat? When are we to take risks? And when are we to weigh up carefully the pros and cons of a situation before making a decision?

Although Peter stepped out in bold faith on many future occasions (for example, the healing of the temple beggar, Acts 3), as far as we know, he never again got out of a boat and walked on water. Are miracles of this kind once-in-a-lifetime events, or should we be expecting

direct divine intervention as a matter of course? Would a
greater abundance of miracles in our lives and in our
churches be proof of a strong faith, or evidence of a weak
faith that needs propping up by signs and wonders?

In the next chapter we will look at two further, but
very different examples of faith. But before we do so, it
is worth pondering the word 'faith' itself.

Bible faith

The Bible word 'faith' (*pistis* in New Testament Greek)
has a range of meanings. The noun is linked to the verb
'to believe' (*pisteuo*), meaning 'to accept or give assent to
a set of beliefs'. The apostle Paul and others frequently
refer to '*the* faith' (1 Tim 3:9; 4:1,6; 5:8; 6:10,12,21),
meaning 'the agreed Christian doctrine or the gospel
truth accepted and proclaimed by the church'.
Whenever we recite the creed, we are reaffirming our
assent to '*the* faith'. But the Bible makes it clear that
mental assent to accepted Christian truth is only one
part of faith. James, a prominent Christian in Jerusalem
and most probably a half-brother to the Lord Jesus,
says, 'You believe that there is one God. Good! Even the
demons believe that – and shudder' (James 2:19).
Believing the water could hold him up was no use to
Peter unless he could actually trust that Jesus had the
power to make it happen.

The story is told of Blondin, the great tightrope
walker, who regularly walked across Niagara Falls. On
one occasion he asked a watching crowd if they believed
he could take another person across in a wheelbarrow.
They all enthusiastically said, 'Yes!' But when he asked

for a volunteer to step forward and into the barrow, the crowd fell strangely silent. At last, a little grey-haired lady came out from the crowd, got in and allowed herself to be pushed across the Falls by Blondin. This lady was his mother!

The third ingredient of faith is obedience. Obedience builds on trust. As the old hymn puts it: 'Trust and obey, for there's no other way, to be happy in Jesus, but to trust and obey'. Peter obeyed when he got out of the boat; Noah obeyed when he built the ark (Gen 6); Abraham obeyed when he left Haran for an unknown destination (Gen 12:1,4); Moses obeyed when he stretched out his arm towards the Red Sea, believing it would part before him (Exod 14:21–22); Joshua obeyed when he stepped into the River Jordan, trusting that it too would part (Josh 3). There are many such examples.

Faith without the evidence of obedient deeds is dead and useless (James 2:18,20,26). Faith is not faith until it results in obedience. To illustrate this to his disciples, Jesus once told a brief parable:

> 'There was a man who had two sons. He went to the first and said, "Son, go and work today in the vineyard."
>
> ' "I will not," he answered, but later he changed his mind and went.
>
> 'Then the father went to the other son and said the same thing. He answered, "I will, sir," but he did not go.
>
> 'Which of the two did what his father wanted?'
>
> 'The first,' they answered.
>
> (Matthew 21:28–31)

Yet another meaning of faith is 'endurance', or 'faith-fulness'. This is the quality of long-term loyalty and commitment. Marriage is intended to be a faithful relationship, a commitment to one person, forsaking all others. The Bible repeatedly describes God as being faithful to his people and requiring their faithfulness in return. Ruth and Zechariah, our subjects for the next chapter, are good examples of faithfulness in trying circumstances. Sometimes faith will not be something dramatic but, rather, expressed in what scripture calls 'patient endurance' (2 Cor 1:6; Rev 1:9; 13:10; 14:12).

Mustard seed faith

A Bible passage that has long troubled me – and frankly still does – is Matthew 17:20–21. This incident occurs just after Jesus' transfiguration. He had taken Peter, James and John up a mountain to pray, and while there they glimpsed his divine glory – his 'otherness' (more on this in chapter three). Meanwhile, at the foot of the mountain, the remaining nine disciples were having difficulty casting a demon out of a young boy. On his return, Jesus chided them for their lack of faith:

> 'I tell you the truth, if you have faith as small as a mustard seed, you can say to this mountain, "Move from here to there" and it will move. Nothing will be impossible for you.'

As far as I know, no-one has ever moved a mountain by prayer. What Jesus is saying is that even an unimpressively small faith can grow and eventually attempt an impossibly large task. This is because our faith doesn't actually do anything of itself. Our faith cannot move a mountain. But God can. As someone has said, 'It is not a great faith in God that we need, but faith in a great God.'

Faith is like a lever or a jack that enables a huge weight to be lifted with very little effort. Imagine a lorry with a puncture. It would be impossible for even the world's strongest man to lift the wheel off the ground. But, with the right jack, even a child could raise the axle to allow a new tyre to be fitted.

Often, we think of faith as something we either have or don't have. But it is not like that – we have all got a degree of faith. Although the mustard seed was the smallest seed known to Palestinian farmers, it grew into a huge, tree-like shrub, as much as five metres high and three metres across, 'so that the birds of the air come and perch in its branches' (Matt 13:32).

Faith can grow, but like us it needs food and exercise if it is to grow. Many things feed faith: the recognition of God's greatness when we worship him; the testimony of other Christians; our giving attention to God's word (Rom 10:17). Faith also grows through exercise, that is, through constant practice. Developing latent gifts, taking on new responsibilities both inside and outside the church, taking steps of faith – often small but sometimes large – will all help to strengthen our trust in God. Unless regularly stretched, our spiritual muscles are likely to get weak and waste away.

Faith will often be mixed with doubt, as it was for Peter on the water and for the father of the demonised boy, waiting for Jesus at the foot of the mountain. Mark, in his account of the same story, records the

father's honest words: 'Lord, I believe, help me overcome my unbelief' (Mark 9:24). But doubt need not
worry us too much. The man did bring his son to Jesus;
Peter did get out of the boat. Obedience is more important than feelings. As William Carey, the pioneering
nineteenth-century Baptist missionary to India, once
said, 'Expect great things from God; attempt great
things for God.'

Chapter Two

A YOUNG WIDOW AND AN OLD MAN

The story of Peter walking on the water has a great deal to teach us about faith, but it by no means exhausts the subject. As we saw in the last chapter, there are many kinds of faith. There is faith like Peter's, which is exercised in a split-second decision, but there is also the faith that is spread over a lifetime. The Bible words 'faith' and 'faithfulness' can conjure up very different pictures in our minds, but they are actually very close in meaning. When we think of 'faith', we may think of doing bold, daring, heroic acts for God – of Moses parting the Red Sea, Daniel in the lion's den and his three friends in the fiery furnace. But when we think of 'faithfulness', we may think of long years of loyal service, possibly with little excitement or adventure and nothing happening that is out of the ordinary or particularly spectacular. But the words 'faith' and 'faithfulness' come from the same root, both in English and in the original languages of the Bible. Faith and faithfulness are one and the same. In fact, unless we are exercising faithfulness (in the sense of long-term loyalty) towards God, it is unlikely that we will rise to the occasion and exercise bold, heroic faith should the need arise.

In this chapter we will look briefly at two further examples of faith or faithfulness, that of a young widow and an old man.

Ruth

The delightfully romantic story of Ruth, a young widow from the country of Moab, is recounted in the Old Testament. It is only four chapters long and can be read in ten minutes. Why not do so now? The opening verse tells us that it is set 'in the days when the judges ruled', an unsettled and often violent period of Israel's history.

Famine had forced Elimelech and his wife Naomi to leave Bethlehem and settle in Moab. Their two sons, Mahlon and Kilion, grew up and married two Moabite women, Orpah and Ruth. First Elimelech and then his sons died, leaving Naomi and her daughters-in-law to face life as widows. Naomi's decision was to return to Bethlehem. And while Orpah chose to remain in Moab, Ruth committed herself to accompanying Naomi back to her home town:

> Ruth replied, ... 'Where you go I will go and where you stay I will stay. Your people will be my people and your God my God. Where you die I will die and there I will be buried. May the Lord deal with me, be it ever so severely, if anything but death separates you and me.'
>
> *(Ruth 1:16)*

This was a major step of faith. Ruth was making a lifetime commitment to God and to his people. We could call this *saving* or *converting* faith. Exactly the same kind of commitment is made when a person declares his or her allegiance to Jesus Christ and his church. The Bible calls it many things, for example, being born again (John 3:1–8; 1 Pet 1:23), becoming a child of God (John 1:12) or becoming a new creation in Christ (2 Cor 5:17). Ruth was also changing nationality. When a person becomes a Christian, he or she ceases to be a citizen of this world and becomes a citizen of heaven, leaving the kingdom of spiritual darkness to join the kingdom of light (Col 1:13).

Saving faith is the most important kind we can ever exercise. Our eternal destiny depends on it. Some people can name the place or give the date and time of their commitment to Jesus Christ (for example, Paul on the road to Damascus, Acts 9). Many more cannot – for them the process is much more gradual. However, what is important is that we can all now say, 'I belong to Jesus; I am his lifelong disciple.'

Unless we have made that step of saving faith, it is a waste of time talking about any other type of faith. If you are not sure whether you truly belong to Christ and have received his gift of eternal life, you should talk this over with a church leader or a trusted Christian friend as soon as possible.

Sometimes evangelists and preachers give the false impression that becoming a Christian is easy and cost-free. While the advantages far outweigh the disadvantages, there is a cost involved. Saving faith involves repentance as well as belief. This is the essential message of the gospel: 'Repent and believe the good news' (Mark 1:15). It means turning away from everything we know that displeases God, asking forgiveness for our wrongdoing and actively choosing to live God's way instead of ours.

Ruth gave up a great deal when she told Naomi, 'Your people will be my people and your God my God.' No longer would she worship Moabite gods such as Chemosh; from now on she would worship only the Lord God of Israel. As well as exchanging a bad religion for a better one (Chemosh was a cruel god whose rituals included child sacrifice), she was letting go of customs that were deeply rooted in her cultural identity as a Moabite – it was unlikely she would ever be accepted back. She was committing herself to an unknown future – as a Moabite, she had little idea how she would be treated in Israel (the Moabites and Israelites were enemies at this time); and as a widow she would be very vulnerable. Journeying to Bethlehem, Ruth would have been aware that there was no certainty she would find a roof over her head or food on her table. She was throwing herself completely on the kindness of God and the generosity of his people.

Ruth's faith did not stop with her expression of saving faith; she exercised faith in other ways too. Having made a commitment to the Lord God, and encouraged by her mother-in-law Naomi, Ruth put her faith in the promises of God's Word. This is important: faith should always rest on the truths of scripture. As the story of Ruth unfolds, we see her taking advantage of two provisions set out in God's law handed down from Moses. They may seem obscure to us, but to an agricultural nation with a land-based economy, they were vitally important for the maintenance of a just and fair society and the eradication of poverty.

The first is the law of gleaning (Lev 23:22). This

required farmers, when gathering in their grain, to leave 'gleanings' – the corners or edges of their fields, or any grain that had been dropped during harvesting – on the ground for the poor to collect. (The poor included foreigners, widows and orphans.) Farmers who complied with this law would be especially blessed by God (Deut 24:19). Prompted by Naomi, Ruth gathered up the grain dropped by harvesters in the fields belonging to one Boaz, a kinsman of Naomi's late husband, Elimelech. Notice that faith rarely excuses us from hard work: Ruth was industrious, working all day with hardly a break except on Boaz's insistence (Ruth 2:14).

The second law of which Ruth took advantage is a little more complicated: it is the law of Levirate marriage (Deut 25:5–10, see also Matt 22:23–28). If a man died leaving a childless widow, his brother or next closest male relative was required to marry the woman. The man fulfilling this duty was known as the *kinsman-redeemer*. This law ensured a number of things: the widow would be protected; the first husband's name would be continued if the remarried widow then bore a son (who would take the dead man's name); and any fields or other property would be kept in the family. Any agreements made had to be witnessed publicly and approved by the local elders. These deals were often agreed by the symbolic exchange of a sandal (Ruth 4:7).

Sometimes faith is passive and we can only wait to see what God will do. But very often there are steps we can take. Ruth and Naomi now give evidence of what we might call *enterprising* faith. Boaz had shown unusual kindness towards Ruth and, as a relative of Naomi's late husband, he qualified as a possible kinsman-redeemer.

But he needed a nudge in the right direction. So Naomi sends Ruth out, showered, perfumed and dressed in her most alluring outfit, to seek out Boaz while he is sleeping near the store of grain that had been threshed that day. Following Naomi's instructions, Ruth wakes him and asks him to fulfil his duty as kinsman-redeemer and marry her. Perhaps it was a leap year!

There is boldness in the women's actions, even a touch of scheming and feminine wiliness. They were prepared to play their part in finding an answer to their prayers. Generally speaking, if there is something we can do to answer our prayers, then we should be doing it with all the boldness and wisdom at our disposal. But, having exercised enterprising faith, Ruth and Naomi then left the outcome in God's hands. This is *passive* or *waiting* faith.

There is a further twist in the tale: an unnamed male relative, closer to Naomi's family than Boaz, must be given first refusal. He was attracted by the prospect of gaining extra land, but not so sure about taking on responsibility for Ruth and thereby bequeathing his property to any children she might have alongside his own children. But Naomi tells Ruth to wait: 'Just be patient and don't worry' (Ruth 3:18, CEV).

In many ways, it is much harder to exercise passive faith than it is to exercise active faith. We don't like not being in control, not having the power to do something to affect the outcome of a decision that involves us. We all know how hard it is to relax while the dentist or doctor tells us to trust him, or to wait for the results of an exam, a job interview or a medical test. We have our part to play – working hard at our studies, preparing the best we can for the interview, or guarding our health through taking sensible precautions about diet and lifestyle; but when the waiting comes, this can be a real test of patience and faith in God.

The story of Ruth has a happy ending. She got her man, a secure future and her place in the history books by becoming the great-grandmother of Israel's most revered monarch, King David.

Zechariah and Elizabeth

From the story of Ruth we learn about the different kinds of faith, both active and passive. We also discover the all-important principle that faith should rest on the truth and promises of God's Word made known in the Bible. For further examples of different kinds of faith, we turn now to the story of Zechariah and his wife Elizabeth (Luke 1). Whenever faith is present, doubt is usually not far away (remember Peter?). Zechariah's story is important in helping us to understand doubt and faith.

Zechariah and Elizabeth were childless, a cause for great pain and sadness both now and then, but in Bible times it was felt especially important to have children – they were a sign of God's blessing and an insurance for old age (there were no pensions or state benefits then). However, Zechariah and Elizabeth were about to become the parents of John the Baptist.

Whenever this story is told, attention is usually drawn to Zechariah's lack of faith. When the angel Gabriel appeared to him, we are told, he was 'startled and gripped with fear' (v 12). Then, on learning that

Elizabeth would bear them a son, he voiced his doubt:
'How will I know this is going to happen? My wife and
I are both very old' (v 18, CEV). For his lack of faith,
Zechariah was struck dumb until baby John was born.

When the angel announced to Mary that she would
be giving birth to Jesus, Mary expressed similar doubts;
she was frightened and 'troubled', and doubted the
truth of his promise: 'How can this be?' (vs 29,34).
Zechariah's doubts were based on his old age and steril-
ity, Mary's on her youth and virginity; but the difference between them lies in this: while Mary was certainly
not praying for a child, Zechariah was.

In both cases, doubt and fear gave way to faith.
Mary, after hearing what God had done for Elizabeth,
declared herself to be the Lord's servant (v 38).
Zechariah went home, enjoyed sexual union with his
wife and she conceived. Mary, at least, was given a sign
– that of Elizabeth's near-geriatric pregnancy – to
encourage her own faith. Zechariah had no such advantage, except, of course, that as a priest he would have
known the promises of the Old Testament. Here again,
we see the importance of knowing and resting upon
God's Word. Two stories would have been particularly
poignant for Zechariah: the angelic visitation to the elderly Abraham, promising him a son through his similarly elderly and barren wife, Sarah (Gen 18:1–15); and the
birth, to the barren Hannah, of Samuel whose life from
childhood was dedicated to service in God's house
under the schooling of Eli the priest (1 Sam 1–3).

So why was Zechariah struck dumb if he was, in
fact, no more doubting than Mary? It seems, from a
careful reading of the story, that it was as much a posi-

tive sign for those waiting outside the temple as it was a negative rebuke to Zechariah himself. For over 400 years, since the time of Malachi, there had been no prophetic revelation, no word from God. Many Jews, especially the scribes and Pharisees, believed that the age of prophecy was now forever closed and the spirit of revelation withdrawn. They no longer expected to hear God's voice, but believed their duty was simply to apply and keep God's law in all its detail, constantly interpreting and reinterpreting it for each successive generation.

This begs another question: Why did God send Gabriel to Zechariah and not some other hapless priest? Was it perhaps because the sense of expectation that others had lost was still alive, somewhere, in Zechariah? Paralleling Mary's song known as the Magnificat (Luke 1:45–55), we have an equally wonderful song from Zechariah (vs 68–79), which is generally known as the Benedictus (meaning 'the Praise-be') after its opening words in Latin.

These words were nine months in the shaping. Zechariah had plenty of time to reflect not only on what God was doing for him and Elizabeth personally, but also on what God was doing for the entire nation of Israel. For nearly half a millennium the heavens had been silent; Zechariah was one of the first to become aware that this silence was about to be broken. His prophetic song, so full of faith, anticipates some of the far-reaching consequences of the new revelation of God which would be ushered in through the birth of John the Baptist, and which would find its climax in the birth, life, death and resurrection of Jesus Christ.

The Benedictus is steeped in the language and imagery of the Old Testament. There are allusions to at least seven books of the Old Testament (Genesis, Numbers, Samuel, Psalms, Isaiah, Micah and Malachi). Genuine faith always rests on God's Word and an awareness of what he has done in the past; yet it is also open to God doing something new and unique in the present. Notice how Zechariah's song moves from the general sweep of God's purposes (vs 68–75) to specific detail about John the Baptist and his future work as the forerunner of the Messiah (vs 76–79). Genuine faith takes in the grand, visionary scale, yet can also see God in action in the detail.

As we saw in the previous chapter, faith is often, rightly, equated with obedience. But we must also equate faith with *expectation*. We can *expect* God to act – maybe not today, maybe not tomorrow, maybe not even in our lifetimes, but act he will. The challenge is this: Can he act through us? Do we expect him to be at work in our world? Do we expect him to be at work in and through our lives?

Let's look more closely at Zechariah and find out what we can learn about what we might call *expectant* faith. Luke takes pains to tell us that this aged but godly priest belonged to the division of Abijah, one of twenty-four such divisions (Luke 1:5; 1 Chron 23–24). Each division served in the temple twice a year for a week at a time and at special festivals. On this occasion, however, Zechariah was chosen by the drawing of lots to be the one priest who would place fresh incense twice daily on the altar inside the Holy of Holies (Exod 30:1–10). To undertake this holy duty was a high privilege which fell to a priest only once in his lifetime, if ever. Just as Ruth worked hard in the fields, so Zechariah took his duties seriously. He would have been concerned to fulfil them to the very best of his ability. Everything had to be done by the book, but the right attitude was also required. Zechariah knew that God looked on the heart as well as on outward actions.

It was as he was performing this holy and delicate task that the angel Gabriel appeared. Although Zechariah was rigid with fear, the angel was kind enough to point first to his faith, not his doubt: 'your prayer has been heard'. But what prayer was this? The set prayers that Zechariah would have been expected to recite on behalf of the nation as part of his temple duty? Yes, certainly. But God had also heard Zechariah's private and very personal prayer – his prayer for himself and Elizabeth, that one day they would have a child. Despite his disappointment and advancing years, he had not allowed hope to die. Perhaps this was a prayer he offered more out of routine than faith. Perhaps, as he and Elizabeth grew older, it was whispered more often than spoken. But always there was hope. Always there was expectation. Always there was faith. And now God was honouring that faith.

The temple, however, was not the place for a priest to offer such personal prayers. There Zechariah would have prayed for the coming of the Messiah, the one who would redeem God's people, rescue them from their oppressors and bind them back to God in a loving covenant relationship. Just as Zechariah held onto a little piece of hope that God would give him a child, so also he held onto the hope that God would one day break the

silence of the heavens and come down, bringing the
Messiah into human view. The wonderful thing is that
both this set prayer and Zechariah's private prayer were
answered in the same instant. God had plans to give
Zechariah the child he wanted *and* he had plans that this
child would be the prophetic forerunner of none other
than the Messiah, the Christ.

Faith has as much to do with long-suffering faithfulness as it has to do with instant obedience. It has as
much to do with commitment and duty as it has to do
with inspiration and enthusiasm. We can draw many
important lessons from Zechariah's actions, but for now
notice just this one thing. At the most privileged point
in his career, Zechariah was nevertheless still in pain,
the pain of childlessness. But he does not allow that pain
to turn to bitterness. Instead, he faithfully goes about
his duties, all the while keeping hope and expectation
alive both for himself and, on a wider perspective, for all
God's people. To be sure, when God responded,
Zechariah was not entirely ready, but would you or I be
if an angel appeared in church one day, announcing that
our prayers had been answered in the most wonderful,
far-reaching, mind-stretching way possible?!

But faith, of whatever kind, whether exercised in an
instant or maintained over a lifetime, has two ends –
ours and God's. Up until now, we have been looking at
the human end. Now it is time to look from God's viewpoint, and to explore something of his relationship with
his world and with us, his creatures.

Chapter Three

GOD AND THE NATURAL WORLD

How we exercise faith, and the kind of faith we exercise, is shaped by what we believe about the way God works in his world. It is precisely at this point that many Christians come unstuck. Our faith rests on God, but if our picture of God is distorted – like a reflection in a fairground hall of mirrors – then our faith is not going to hold together.

My wife and I once thought of buying an old timbered cottage. It had stood for three hundred years, but we were not at all sure it would stand for three more. Its walls were bowing outward, none of the downstairs rooms was entirely square and upstairs the bedroom floors had a distinct slope to them! Walking from room to room felt rather like being inside one of those 'crazy houses' found at a funfair: the disorientation made us feel uncomfortably off-balance. The owners explained it was because the foundations had moved over the centuries. Despite assurances we would soon get used to everything being at odd angles, we decided to look elsewhere. If the foundations of a house are faulty or not deep enough, then sooner or later this will show above

ground. The same is true of our faith. Everything may
fit together when life is going well, but when suffering
or setback tests the foundations, cracks will sooner or
later start to appear.

To understand how God works in his world and
interacts with it, we must start with what the Bible has
to say about creation.

God and creation

Some see God as a volcano, occasionally erupting into
violent action but dormant and inactive the rest of the
time. Such a view (technically it is called *deism*) falls
woefully short of the biblical and Christian understanding of how God works in his world. It is, nevertheless,
the model by which, in practice, a large number of
Christians live their lives for much of the time.

The 'volcano' model goes like this. Having set the
universe in motion, God leaves it alone to operate
according to the laws he has laid down. For much of the
time he allows the universe to run itself, leaving us to
make the best of our circumstances. As though sleeping
with an eye half open and an ear half listening, God
notes the affairs of the world and the comings and
goings of its people, but, for all intents and purposes, he
may as well be fast asleep. However, just occasionally he
wakes up and erupts into action. This might be because
he has decided to act out of his sovereign will, either to
bless the godly or – more likely we suspect – to smite the
ungodly. Alternatively, he might lumber into action
because he has been prodded into doing so by the
prayers of his people, provided, of course, they have

prayed in the right way with the right motives and with the right amount of faith and fervour.

Such a view of God, far from being Christian, is in fact a pagan one. Any approach to this kind of god is made not out of faith but from fear and superstition. The story of Elijah's contest with the prophets of Baal on Mount Carmel ideally illustrates this (1 Kings 18). The worshippers of Baal believed their god could only be woken if the prayers of his devotees were loud and fervent enough. All day long several hundred of them prayed, becoming ever more frenzied in their devotion, ranting and raving, even inflicting violence upon themselves in their attempt to wake their drowsing god. Their efforts were mocked by Elijah: 'You'll have to shout louder than that to catch the attention of your god. Perhaps he is talking to someone, or is sitting on the toilet, or maybe he is away on a trip, or is asleep and needs to be wakened' (v 28, LB).

A god who erupts into action only when it suits him, or when his followers shout loud enough, is a god who is volatile, changeable, capricious, even malicious. He hears the prayers of some, but not others. He has favourites and acts on whims. He keeps his servants – or should we call them slaves? – guessing, uncertain as to whether or not they will find him in a receptive mood.

There are two great failings of this 'volcano' model as a means of understanding how our God – the God and Father of our Lord Jesus Christ – works in the world. First, as we have seen, it reduces him to the level of a pagan deity no better than Baal. Second, it casts serious doubt on his goodness and love. Although God's ways are higher than our ways, his thoughts higher than our thoughts (Isaiah 55:8–9), his wisdom unfathomable and his will beyond our comprehension, it is nevertheless clear, both from scripture and mature reflection on personal experience, that to picture God behaving in a volcano-like fashion is woefully short of the truth.

Psalm 121 is just one of many Bible passages to which we could turn to see the inadequacy of this model. In the psalm, the writer is on a journey, quite probably a journey of pilgrimage from his home town to Jerusalem, where he intends to worship God in the temple. Evidently, the journey is long and arduous, taking the psalmist through dangerous mountain terrain. There are both natural and human perils. There is danger from the scorching heat of the midday sun; there is danger from the freezing night air; there is danger from bandits; and there is the simple weariness of a long and tiring journey. The psalmist looks to the hills. They remind him of how far he has yet to travel and of the perils that might lurk around every corner. But they also speak to him of the might and majesty of God. If God put these mountains in place, surely he can look after the needs of those travelling through them.

Creator and Sustainer

In many books on Christian doctrine, the chapter on God as Creator is one of the briefest. The authors seem to want to move on as quickly as possible to what they regard as more meaty subjects, such as 'God as Saviour and Redeemer'. But many of our questions about faith, discernment, prayer, healing, guidance and so forth, are questions we cannot begin to answer until we have a right understanding of God as the Creator and Sustainer of the universe. The writer of Psalm 121 begins here, affirming his belief in the God who is Maker of all things, Lord of creation, who sustains all things by his power (v 2).

The Bible repeatedly affirms that God not only made the world but also actively sustains its existence by his power:

> The Son is the radiance of God's glory and the exact representation of his being, *sustaining all things by his powerful word*.
>
> *(Hebrews 1:3, my italics)*

> He is the image of the invisible God, the firstborn over all creation. For by him all things were created: things in heaven and on earth, visible and invisible, whether thrones or powers or rulers or authorities; all things were created by him and for him. He is before all things, *and in him all things hold together*.
>
> *(Colossians 1:15–17, my italics)*

Jesus, telling his disciples not to worry about their material needs, reminds them – and us – of God's interest and involvement in creation:

> 'Look at the birds of the air; they do not sow or reap or store away in barns, and yet your heavenly Father feeds them ... See how the lilies of the field grow. They do not labour or spin. Yet I tell you that not even Solomon in all his splendour was dressed like one of these.'
>
> *(Matthew 6:26–29)*

Five times in Psalm 121 the psalmist says that God 'watches' (NIV); alternative translations are 'keeps'

(NRSV), 'guards' (REB) or 'protects' (CEV). This does not depict passivity; rather, to guard or protect is to do something active. So, as well as being above and beyond all things, God is intimately and actively involved in his creation. He is both Creator *and* Sustainer. He has not left the universe running on automatic pilot.

We can summarise the Bible's teaching on God as Creator and Sustainer as follows:

- God made everything from nothing (Heb 11:3). This includes both the material world that is visible to us and the spiritual world that is invisible.

- The world is separate from God. It is not a part of him nor an extension of him. Nevertheless, creation is entirely dependent on God for its continued existence.

- What we know of God is completely dependent on his revealing himself to us.

- God is greater than his creation and independent of it. He is over, outside and beyond it. Theologians call this the 'transcendence' or 'otherness' of God.

- However, God is not removed or at a distance from his creation. He is everywhere and always present. We call this the 'immanence' or 'nearness' of God.

We can now explore these last two aspects in more detail.

The 'otherness' and 'nearness' of God

God dwells in eternity. He is not limited by time or

space. He is all-powerful and all-knowing. (Theologians speak of God's 'omnipotence' and 'omniscience' respectively.) He is therefore beyond our human understanding and our human grasp. We cannot probe him with our scientific instruments; we cannot put him under the microscope or search for him through a telescope. But he is also close to every one of us and intimately involved in the universe he has made. This, however, does not restrict his freedom nor does it take away ours.

God is not only the Creator of the world, he is also its Sustainer. He did not set the universe in motion and then abandon it to its fate (deism). In creation, we see God's constant and continued care for all that he made. This is possible because he has made the world an orderly place. The sun rises and sets regularly 'on the evil and the good', 'the righteous and the unrighteous' (Matt 5:45); the tilt of the earth maintains the climate and the seasons on which our food depends (Acts 14:17). We call this abundant generosity of God to all his creatures, his 'providence'.

The entire Bible is the record of God's involvement in his creation:

In his hand is the life of every living thing
and the breath of every human being.
(Job 12:10, NRSV)

'For in him we live and move and have our being.'
(Acts 17:28)

These verses stress God's nearness and creation's continual dependency on him. And both the nearness and the otherness of God are asserted when the apostle Paul

speaks of the 'one God and Father of all, who is over all
and through all and in all' (Eph 4:6).

Those who stress the otherness of God to the exclusion of his nearness are likely to emphasise the importance of his occasional interventions into the natural
order of things. They see God (to put it in theological
language!) zapping us with his power from on high,
either to help or to menace. God could be likened to an
orbiting satellite, ordinarily out of view, but with the
power to strike any point on earth at will with a blast of
his energy. Displays of God's transcendent power may
be more or less frequent, depending on whether one
believes that miracles and other divine dramatic interventions are likely to be very rare or near-daily events.
(We will look at this further in the next chapter.)

On the other hand, those who stress the nearness of
God are more likely to see him at work through the
ordinary rather than the extraordinary. They emphasise
his provision of our daily needs, his working through
happy coincidences, 'chance' meetings, other people,
perfect timing and particular combinations of circumstances. God thus becomes a kind of behind-the-scenes
stage-manager who moves the furniture around without
us being very much aware of it, unless we have the 'eye
of faith' to see what he is doing.

Neither picture is right or wrong as such.
Sometimes, from our limited human perspective, we
will be more aware of God's otherness; at other times we
will be more aware of his nearness. But in truth, God is
always 'other' and always 'near' at the same time. The
writer of Psalm 121 understood both these aspects of
God's being and was able to hold them in balance in his

mind. To his way of thinking, God is the Maker of heaven and earth, the all-powerful one who stands over and beyond his creation. Yet, at the same time, God is also the pslamist's constant companion and guardian, overseeing all his comings and goings, closer to him than his own right arm (vs 5,8).

The difficulty comes when we lose the balance and stress the otherness of God to the exclusion of his nearness, or vice-versa. Christians who want to believe only in the transcendent power of God may be unable to see him at work in quieter, less dramatic circumstances. Likewise, those who take refuge in the thought of God's nearness may never pray for, let's say, a miracle of healing or may run a mile from the activities of some of their more charismatic friends. Christians who always expect a miracle may find their faith threatened when none seems evident. They may feel stuck in the boat when they want to be climbing overboard to walk on the water. Similarly, Christians who are only comfortable when God goes about things more prosaically may feel threatened when the time comes for them to take the risky step of climbing out of the boat.

Suffering and the goodness of God

There is, however, a rather nasty fly in the ointment: if God in his otherness is all-powerful and in his nearness all-loving, why is there suffering in the world he has made? Even if we accept that the 'volcano' model is all wrong and God is in fact both Creator and Sustainer, both near and far, and not at all like the mercurial pagan god Baal who had to be prodded into action, why does it sometimes feel that this is precisely the way life is?

Sometimes experience points to the goodness of God – an answer to prayer, success in some venture, a miracle of healing, everything in life coming together for a moment of unspoilt joy. At other times there is no answer to prayer, failure instead of success, continued illness instead of a miracle, disappointment instead of joy. Few of us get beyond our earliest childhood without knowing pain as well as joy. Frankly, can we believe in a consistently good God?

We will look at the problem of suffering in a later chapter on healing, but I want to share with you a personal experience through which I learnt important and lasting lessons about the goodness of God.

My wife and I were in the doctor's consulting room. 'I'm sorry to have to tell you,' he said, 'but you will never have your own children.' We left numb and uncomprehending. Within a few days, shock gave way to anger. Sarah went out into the garden and shouted to the skies: 'Why, God? Why?' There was no reply. The heavens remained silent.

We began working through our options. Without children in tow, did God perhaps want us to go on the mission field? Did he perhaps want us to foster other people's children, or adopt our own? We asked for guidance from a wise Christian leader who came to our church to conduct a weekend conference. Seeing our anger, he suggested we planned nothing and did nothing until we had placed the matter in God's hands and left it there. Over the coming weeks we wrestled in prayer until we were genuinely able to let go and trust in the same way Job had when he said, 'Though he slay me, yet will I hope in him' (Job 13:15). To say such a prayer is not fatalism, a shrugging of the shoulders in cold indifference; rather, it is to trust in the essential goodness of God, to believe that he loves me, that he knows better than I do what is the very best for my life.

The same positive expression of relinquishment is found in the prayer of commitment made during the Methodist Covenant Service:[1]

> I am no longer my own but yours.
> Your will, not mine, be done in all things,
>> wherever you may place me,
>> in all that I do
>>> and in all that I may endure;
>> when there is work for me
>>> and when there is none;
>> when I am troubled
>>> and when I am at peace.
> Your will be done
>> when I am valued
>>> and when I am disregarded;
>> when I find fulfilment
>>> and when it is lacking;
>> when I have all things,
>>> and when I have nothing.
> I willingly offer all I have and am
>> to serve you, as and where you choose.

Today, we have two children and three grandchildren. The full story would take too long to tell. Suffice to say, it involved a wonderful and rapid series of answers to prayer, culminating in our being accepted as suitable adoptive parents within an unusually short space of time. In the final interview of the process we were asked to offer a profile of the child or children we wanted to

adopt. We took a bold step of faith. We said we wanted
to adopt children in one of the designated special needs
categories, namely, children over five years of age, who
are considered harder to place. But we also said we
wanted them to be under eight and that we wanted not
one but at least two from the same family. Our narrow-
ly-defined request was agreed, but we were told it was
so specific we would probably have to wait many years.
The last time two children had been adopted together in
our district had been fourteen years previously and
they'd been teenagers.

Just three weeks later the phone went. Two children,
sister and brother, aged six and seven respectively, had
become available for adoption in another part of the
country. No suitable home had been found for them
there, so the social workers in our district had been contacted. Did they know of any possible adoptive parents?
They thought they might!

Just eighteen months after the hospital consultant
had pronounced his fateful verdict, Simon and Eva
came into our home. Nine months later we officially
adopted them. Life has had many setbacks since then
(and our children, like most, have brought their share of
headaches as well as joy). But we know beyond doubt
that our God – the God and Father of our Lord Jesus
Christ – is good and loving in all that he does and is.

Jesus, God's Son

Alongside the Christian doctrine of creation, the doctrine
of the *incarnation* provides us with our understanding of
how God in his goodness relates to us, his creatures.

God has at no time become more closely involved in his creation than during the human lifetime of his Son, Jesus Christ. In a draughty stable-cave at Bethlehem, God entered the world in human form. The introduction to John's Gospel (1:1–18) affirms that Mary's son was no less than the eternal Word of God, ever-present with God from before the creation of the world. The babe in the manger was the very one through whom the stars were flung into space, the earth and moon set in their orbits about the sun. Here, in Wesley's words, we see 'our God contracted to a span, incomprehensibly made man'.

Jesus was not schizophrenic: he did not sometimes operate in a divine, 'otherness' mode and at other times in a human, 'nearness' mode. He was at all times fully God and fully human. Occasionally, his divine glory broke through, for example, during his transfiguration (Matt 17:1–8; Mark 9:2–9; Luke 9:28–36). His appearance changed, his face became as bright as the sun and his clothes as white as light. A bright cloud, symbolising God's presence and glory, overshadowed the group.

However, for much of the time, Jesus' divine identity was hidden. He did not, as some paintings suggest, walk around with a halo about his head to indicate he was the Son of God. Yet clues to his divine nature were present for those willing to see them. His miracles were the most obvious: Nicodemus, the Pharisee, observed when he met him, 'Rabbi, we know you are a teacher who has come from God. For no one could perform the miraculous signs you are doing if God were not with him' (John 3:2). Jesus also claimed to have the power to forgive sin and to be one with God, which, to his fellow

Jews, amounted to blasphemy (Mark 2:5–7; John 10:30). And on one occasion he even claimed for himself the title 'I am', the nearest equivalent to the revered Old Testament name for God, the Lord, or Yahweh (John 8:58) – this time he was threatened with death by stoning. Although his disciples acknowledged him to be the Messiah (Matt 16:16; Mark 8:29; Luke 9:20), it was only after his resurrection that they were fully able to recognise and worship him as God (John 20:28).

As well as understanding his fully divine nature, it is important to realise that Jesus was as fully human as he could possibly be. Christians often fall into the trap of thinking – or acting as though they thought – that Jesus was really God but somehow just temporarily or partially disguised as a human being, as though he were wearing a mask which could be discarded when the need arose in order to undertake some miracle or other. In their attempt to be reverent and to indicate Jesus' unique nature as the Son of God, films like Zeffirelli's *Jesus of Nazareth* often portray him as being rather less than human: his hair is never ruffled by the wind; he hardly blinks; he always speaks in measured and pious tones; he seems to float a few inches above the ground.

God underlined for me the human nature of Jesus in an interesting way. Before my ordination to the Baptist ministry, I taught English to overseas students. One of the most lively came from Mexico. His name was Jesus (pronounced *hay-zous* in Spanish). He was a likeable character with an infectious smile, but prone to mischief. I was constantly telling Jesus to sit down, open his textbook, or pay attention instead of daydreaming out of the window! Although the Bible asserts that Jesus, God's

Son, was sinless (Heb 4:15), this surely cannot mean he was always deadly serious and never having any fun or enjoying life. If he was like that, he would have come across as aloof, dull and boring! Jesus was no party-pooper; in fact, he was a regular partygoer. If only some Christians could grasp that fact! How many Christians imagine that in order to be more spiritual they have somehow to become less human? How many take them-selves too seriously and, as a result, are the most boring people to be with? Sadly, thousands do and are.

Soon after I became a Christian, I was greatly helped by a retired lady in our church. For a while 'Birdie' and I prayed together on a weekly basis. One day she prayed what at the time I thought was a rather strange prayer: she prayed that I would be naturally spiritual and spiri-tually natural. Nowadays I often look back with grati-tude for her wisdom and her prayers, though I am not so sure that particular one has been answered as fully as it might in the twenty-five years since she prayed it. Even today I all too often take myself too seriously. I still catch myself feeling slightly guilty if I am not busily engaged in some 'spiritual' activity. I still need to learn that being more spiritual does not mean being less human. In fact, it means being more fully human, more fully the person God intends me to be.

We have this horrible habit of compartmentalising our lives. We can relate to God in some of them: he is with us in church, in our Bible studies and in our cho-sen sphere of Christian ministry. But we fail to see his Spirit's presence and activity in other parts of our lives: our work, our leisure activities, our relationship with non-Christians (except, of course, when we might be witnessing to them!), our spending (except, again, the tithe or whatever we might put in the offering). We will pick up on some of these issues in Part 2 of this book, but if our understanding of God as Creator and Sustainer teaches us anything, it should teach us that he is as much involved in our secular work as he is in our Christian ministry, as much in our relationships with unbelievers as with believers, as much in our everyday world as our church life, as much in our sorrows as in our joys, as much in our failures as our successes.

To summarise then: in this chapter I have asserted that God is over and above and beyond his creation. Precisely because he is outside his creation (his 'otherness') while at the same time he is everywhere present within it (his 'nearness'), he is able to enter into a meaningful relationship with us, the people he has made. This he has done supremely in the person of his Son, Jesus Christ.

✑ Note

1. *Methodist Worship Book*, Methodist Publishing, 1999, p288.

Chapter Four

GOD AND THE SUPERNATURAL

In the previous chapter we examined our understanding of how God works in the world he has made and is sustaining by his power. But behind and beyond the world we know through our physical senses (sight, hearing, smell, taste and touch) there is another realm that is largely invisible to us – the spiritual, or supernatural, world. A story that may help us understand this is found in 2 Kings 6.

Israel and Syria (or Aram in some Bible translations) were at war. Several times Elisha the prophet was able to warn the King of Israel whenever the King of Syria planned to ambush him. As a result, the Syrian king decided it was time to do away with the prophet. Discovering Elisha was in Dothan, he took an army and surrounded the city under cover of darkness:

> When the servant of the man of God got up and went out early the next morning, an army with horses and chariots had surrounded the city. 'Oh, my lord, what shall we do?' the servant asked.
>
> 'Don't be afraid,' the prophet answered. 'Those who are with us are more than those who are with them.'

> And Elisha prayed, 'O LORD, open his eyes so that he
> may see.' Then the LORD opened the servant's eyes, and
> he looked and saw the hills full of horses and chariots of
> fire all round Elisha.
>
> *(2 Kings 6:15-17)*

Outflanking the Syrian chariots and warhorses was an
even stronger heavenly army of angelic charioteers!

Let's be clear about what was happening. It was not
that the angelic army suddenly appeared when Elisha
prayed: it was there the whole time the city was under
threat. But the presence of this army was invisible to
ordinary sight. Elisha was praying that his servant might
be able to see what the prophet himself already knew to
be the reality.

> Faith is being sure of what we hope for and certain of
> what we do not see.
>
> *(Hebrews 11:1)*

I once saw an angel. Well, very nearly. I was with a
group of young people involved in a summer mission in
Stockholm, Sweden. Among the group was a Christian
from Egypt with whom I shared accommodation. The
only place available for the two of us to sleep was the
floor of the church we were using as a centre.

One afternoon, our entire group was in the church
praying for our evening outreach. My Egyptian brother
in Christ announced that he could see a tall, shining figure standing in the church doorway, as though guarding
the building. None of the rest of us saw anything. Part
of me was not sure I believed him; another part was
envious that he had seen something while I had not.

That night we were sleeping on our mattresses on the floor close to a window. We were woken by a noise just above our heads. We cautiously raised our heads above the windowsill and peered out. A man was attempting to break in by prising the window open with a crowbar. The would-be burglar saw us and left. Reflecting on the incident the following morning, we realised that our angelic visitor the previous afternoon had been a promise of God's protection.

I do not want to get hung up on angels in this chapter. The word 'angel' merely means 'messenger'. The writer of Hebrews tells us that angels are 'only servants ... spirits sent from God to care for those who will receive salvation' (1:14, NLT). Far more wonderful than any protection they might give us is the promise of Jesus' continual presence with us. He promises never to leave or abandon us (Josh 1:5; Heb 13:5); he has given us his Spirit to dwell within our hearts (John 15:17); and he guarantees that nothing can separate us from the love of God (Rom 8:39). I tell the story of Elisha and my own much lesser experience merely as a reminder that we belong to two worlds – the natural and the supernatural.

At the start of this chapter I made the statement that the supernatural world lies *behind* and *beyond* the natural. This is important. Just as God has the qualities of 'otherness' and 'nearness', so the spiritual or supernatural has these same two qualities. God is Spirit. He is above and separate from his creation, yet his presence permeates every part of it. As the Jesuit poet Gerard Manley Hopkins wrote in 1877, 'The world is charged with the grandeur of God'; and yet, as Solomon recognised in his prayer marking the building of Israel's first temple, 'the heavens, even the highest heaven, cannot contain' him (1 Kings 8:27).

God's revelation of himself

In the previous chapter we saw that what we know of God is completely dependent on his revealing himself to us. Our God is active in his world and speaks to his world. He does so both from outside this world and from inside it.

One defining moment of revelation is the story of God's appearance to Moses from within the burning bush (Exod 3). Here we see God's otherness and nearness at work together. In the dry, hot desert, thornbushes often catch fire spontaneously. There is no miracle in that. The miracle lay in the fact that this bush was not destroyed by the fire. This was less of a miracle *beyond* creation and more of a miracle *behind* it. 'The burning bush was a miracle, but only just; a miracle almost buried within the unmiraculous; a miracle seen only by those who will pay attention.'[1] The supernatural is not un-natural or anti-natural. It is just what the word says it is – *super*natural – meaning above or beyond nature.

We can categorise some of the ways in which God makes himself known. They range from the supernatural to the natural, and all degrees in between.

• A divine or angelic appearance

For example, Moses and the burning bush (Exod 3); the angel Gabriel coming to Mary (Luke 1); Paul on the road to Damascus (Acts 9).

• *An audible voice*

For example, Abraham on Mount Moriah about to sacrifice Isaac (Gen 22); the boy Samuel in the temple (1 Sam 3).

• *Miraculous signs*

For example, all the nature miracles and miracles of healing recorded in the Bible; modern-day examples of healing and other miracles.

The *NIV Thematic Study Bible* defines miracles as 'events that are totally out of the ordinary and that cannot be adequately explained on the basis of natural occurrences'. Signs, it says, are 'given to confirm God's Word. They may warn the rebellious or encourage the faithful.'[2]

It is important to note that miraculous signs can only encourage faith: they can never guarantee or force faith. There are many examples in the Bible of people refusing to believe or obey on the evidence of signs given to them.

• *Dreams and visions*

For example, Joseph and Daniel, both of whom could also interpret the dreams of others; Ezekiel (chapters 1, 8–11, 37, 40–48); Peter on the rooftop in Joppa (Acts 10); Paul, beckoned to 'come over and help' in Europe (Acts 16:9–10); John (Revelation).

• *The gifts of the Spirit*

See chapter six for definitions and a list of examples.

• An inner 'voice'

The Holy Spirit speaks through our thoughts and feelings as we learn to submit them to his will and allow them to be shaped by God's Word. In this way the individual Christian or the Christian community may be said to 'have the mind of Christ' (1 Cor 2:16). This spiritual intuition, as we may call it, is perhaps the most common way, apart from scripture, in which God addresses his people. I will say more about knowing the 'mind of Christ' in the final chapter of this book.

• Another person

The Holy Spirit may also speak to us through the words of other people, especially those within the family of the church. We hope that he speaks to us regularly through the preaching we hear and the teaching we receive. He will also speak to us as we solicit the prayers and seek the wisdom of other Christians, particularly church leaders and those more mature in the faith than ourselves.

This list is by no means intended as exhaustive, but you will see that it ranges from quite supernatural means to those that, from our human viewpoint, we commonly regard as fairly unspectacular. Our trouble is that we have a tendency to think that the more impressive are somehow more important and, therefore, better and more dependable. This is an unsafe conclusion.

There are some principles of which we should be aware, especially in the realm of signs and wonders. First, miracles do not guarantee a response of faith. For instance, the ten plagues that befell the Egyptians only served to harden Pharaoh's heart further each time they happened (Exod 7–11). And many people who initially followed Jesus because of his miracles soon disappeared into the background when he ran into conflict with the authorities. Among the mob who called for his crucifixion must have been some who witnessed his miracles at firsthand.

Second, too great a dependence on, or fascination with, the miraculous can distract us from God. Jesus was frequently concerned that people might believe in him for the wrong reasons. On one occasion he stated that only 'a wicked and adulterous generation looks for a miraculous sign' (Matt 16:4). Miracles are never an end in themselves; they are 'signs', pointers to something greater, namely to Jesus and his kingdom, to the rule and reign of God both now and in the age to come.

Third, though we may pray for miracles, it lies only within the sovereign power of God to dispense or withhold them. Although never altogether absent, miracles seem more concentrated at certain points of Bible history than others. In fact, the Bible records three great periods of miraculous activity: the ministry of Moses; the ministries of Elijah and Elisha; and the ministry of Jesus and the early church.

Fourth, scripture and church history suggest that God, in his sovereign mercy, is more likely to break in with miraculous power *in extremis* – for example, in situations of grave danger or persecution, or pioneering situations in which there is the opportunity for a gospel breakthrough.

Fifth, miracles are given for mission. They are signs given to lead the unbeliever towards faith. It seems to me that many Christians today are looking for evidence of the miraculous to protect and isolate themselves from the pain of the world rather than as a means of engaging compassionately with a hurting world. God blesses the faithful and powerless, not the lazy, with signs of his power. All too often, the church wants a quick-fix for its problems. It is looking for the feel-good factor, for immunity from attack, for a place to hide from the world. God wants to lead us out beyond the relative safety we find inside our churches.

Sixth, and perhaps most important of all, is the truth that God delights to make his power known in weakness. Paul learnt this lesson through his experience of a 'thorn in the flesh' (2 Cor 12:7–10). God told him, 'My grace is sufficient for you; my power is made perfect in weakness.' And Paul responds:

> Therefore I will boast all the more gladly about my weaknesses, so that Christ's power may rest on me. That is why, for Christ's sake, I delight in weaknesses, in insults, in hardships, in persecutions, in difficulties. For when I am weak, then I am strong.

Gentleness, meekness and a servant-heart are the marks of true spirituality, not how many miracles one has performed. Spiritual power comes through brokenness and vulnerability, not spiritual one-upmanship, or the control and manipulation of others through demonstrations of the supernatural. Paul's words cut across much of the cheap triumphalism and super-spirituality found in many Christian circles today.

The birth, life, death and resurrection of Jesus Christ are foundational for all Christian belief. His resurrection was the greatest miracle ever to take place, but it came only after the humility of his birth, the servanthood of his life and the complete brokenness of the cross. Power-hungry Christians are not those who will see more of the supernatural and miraculous in their lives. Power-hungry Christians only want to make themselves invincible. The truly victorious Christian is the one who, like Paul, wants 'to know Christ and the power of his resurrection and the fellowship of sharing in his sufferings', having first become 'like him in his death' (Phil 3:10).

God and the ordinary

Dallas Willard, author of *Hearing God*, suggests that the supernatural and the miraculous are not God's preferred method of communication. He goes on to show how God speaks to us more frequently through the last two means in our list of the ways in which he reveals himself, namely, through our own inner spirit and through other people. He calls these two means, respectively, the primary *subjective* and *objective* ways in which God addresses us. These means, he says, are 'best suited to the purposes of God because [they] *most fully engage the faculties of free, intelligent beings, involved in the work of God as his co-labourers and friends.*'[3] Although less spectacular, these more common-sense means of communication are, in the end, more likely to be life-changing and life-shaping. This is true for several reasons:

- They develop our relationship with God and our trust in him.

- They develop our relationship with others and our trust in them.

- They lead to long-term growth in our knowledge and love of God.

- They lead to maturity – a well-rounded faith and balanced personality.

We have already mentioned the story of Elijah and his contest on Mount Carmel with the prophets of Baal (1 Kings 18). The story contains a memorable Bible miracle: the spontaneous combustion of a water-soaked altar and its offering. But in the very next chapter, there is an equally significant story. Fearful and depressed, Elijah flees for his life. Not for the first time, he is miraculously fed. His heaven-sent meal sustains him physically for forty days but does nothing to revive his spiritual state. Then, on Mount Horeb in the southern extremity of the Sinai desert, he meets God:

> Then a great and powerful wind tore the mountains apart and shattered the rocks before the LORD, but the LORD was not in the wind. After the wind there was an earthquake, but the LORD was not in the earthquake. After the earthquake came a fire, but the LORD was not in the fire. And after the fire came a gentle whisper.
> *(1 Kings 19:11–12)*

The wind, earthquake and fire were all known precursors of God's appearing, but on this occasion he was present in none of these great supernatural spectacles. Instead, he made himself known in 'a gentle whisper' (NIV) or 'still small voice' (KJV). Literally, the phrase means 'the sound (or voice) of thin silence'. On this occasion bigger did not mean better. Despite past events, Elijah had to learn that God did not always operate through the realm of the supernatural. Whether Elijah heard a quiet, but just audible voice, or whether he simply sensed within himself what it was God had to say, we do not know. Either way, he was a grateful recipient of the voice of God through means that were closer to the natural and intuitive than the supernatural.

The right balance

One question remains before we come to the end of what has been a theologically heavy but important chapter. When should we expect God to work in his otherness, coming to us in more supernatural ways? And when should we expect him to work in his nearness, coming to us in the 'gentle whisper' of our own inner spirit, or the advice of a Christian brother or sister? Should we be looking for miracles at the drop of a hat? Angels round every corner? Or does all that belong in the past, to pioneering missionaries, miracle-working evangelists and that church down the road, which, if you believe the reports, God seems to bless Sunday after Sunday in one remarkable way or another? If we did live in that kind of environment, we say to ourselves, we would have great faith. Knowing when to step out of the boat would be easy. Caution and common sense would never have to be applied.

Yet perhaps we must learn to be content with being more like Ruth or Zechariah, plodding on faithfully, happy to know that God is with us in our toil. Then there would be few great leaps of faith, just the consistent application of common sense as we seek to live faithfully according to those Christian principles we know to be sound and certain. As we shall see in Part 2 of this book, God does not intend it to be 'either/or'. It can and should be 'both/and'.

Although it may help us to think of God in his otherness and his nearness – that is, in his supernatural (miraculous) power and natural (non-miraculous) ways of engaging with his creation and with us his creatures – God has one personality, not two. The God we meet in the wind and fire, the angelic visitation or the blinding miracle is the same God who whispers in the thin silence. The Jesus who walked on the waves is the same Jesus who wept at Lazarus' graveside. The Holy Spirit who comes in tongues of pentecostal fire is the same Holy Spirit who puts a simple, childlike joy within the forgiven sinner. Praise be to his name.

✇ Notes

1. Dennis Lennon, *Weak Enough for God to Use*, Scripture Union, 1999, p 10.

2. *New International Version Thematic Study Bible*, Alistair McGrath *et al* (eds), Hodder & Stoughton, 1996, pp 1369, 1373–74.

3. Dallas Willard, *Hearing God*, Fount (an imprint of HarperCollins Publishers), 1999, pp 88, 91 (his italics).

~ *Chapter Five* ~

HEALING, FAITH AND COMMON SENSE

Andrew, a student, was barely in his twenties, yet suffered from arthritis so severely he was having to contemplate leaving university. He made an appointment to see me one week-day and asked if I would pray for his healing. This I was eager to do – until he told me the rest of the story.

He explained that he had been to several churches with the same request and had been prayed for many times, all without apparent result. My faith, not that great to begin with, started to sink like Peter when he saw the wind-tossed waves. I prayed for Andrew more out of pastoral duty than with any sense of faith or expectancy. In the empty church I prayed for his healing, but I played safe and also prayed for inner peace in the event that God might not heal. Andrew left.

A couple of weeks later, he returned. As he approached, I began to rehearse in my mind what I could say to help him come to terms with his lack of healing. He took me entirely by surprise when he announced that he was over ninety per cent better. 'Great,' I said, 'praise the Lord.' But I said it in a measured, matter-of-fact kind of voice which implied, 'Well, that's what I expected all along. Didn't you?' As far as I know, his arthritis never flared up again.

Another story: Richard. He was two, maybe three. One Sunday, we were asked to pray urgently for him. He had been rushed to hospital for an emergency operation to remove a fast-growing and malignant brain tumour. Richard came through the operation, but it had been impossible to remove all the cancer.

The church came together for prayer. Whole evenings were given over to it. Two, three months passed. Richard's future was on a knife-edge, but we began to feel that we might just be winning the battle. Then calamity. The cancer came back with a vengeance and started spreading rapidly again. I went to see Richard and his parents, as I had done many times previously, and, as before, I asked them how they wanted the church to pray. Not now for healing, they said, but for a peaceful end.

It was my task to explain to the church why we had apparently changed tack and were now praying differently. Some said it was wrong to pray this way; others said it showed a lack of faith.

The doctors expected young Richard to live a further three months, perhaps six. Just three weeks later he died peacefully in his grandmother's arms with his parents and family gathered round him. I took his funeral. So many questions.

I preached again the following Sunday, trying to address some of the issues raised. I explained that we are called to love and that love always involves the risk of disappointment. When we pray for healing, it is often not faith that we lack but compassion.

We sang the song by Danny Daniels, 'I am a wounded soldier, but I will not leave the fight.' Would I get so deeply involved again? Yes, I would. Would I do the same all over again? Yes, I would. Would I pray the same way all over again? Again, the answer was still a definite 'yes'.

At the time, our church was just embarking on the healing ministry. A large number of church members had attended a John Wimber conference. John Wimber, leader of the Californian Vineyard Fellowship, had introduced us to the ministry of 'signs and wonders'. Since then we had become accustomed to 'words of knowledge' in our services (see the next chapter for an example), and we had seen several small healings. But Richard was the first real challenge to our new sense of expectancy and faith in God's healing power. We had much to learn.

I am still learning. As I write, Ann, a lady in her forties and one of our church members, is fighting for her life against lung cancer. We have prayed for her and we have prayed with her: we pray for her at almost every church service and prayer meeting, and we pray with her before her monthly dose of chemotherapy. (We are, as it were, giving Ann a course of prayer treatment in parallel to the medical treatment.) There have been some genuine answers to prayer, I believe: Ann has a tremendous sense of peace; she is largely free from pain; God has been at work in her family; and, at the time of writing, she is physically better than at any time in the last six months. (She is, for example, able to take a daily half-hour walk whereas six months ago she was confined to a wheelchair.) But the big one – the miracle of healing – has eluded her.

Ann still has faith. Every time I meet to pray with her, I ask how she wants the church to pray. 'For healing and a deeper relationship with God,' she says. She is not afraid of death. She does not want healing only for her sake, more for the sake of her family. Her brother died of cancer eight years ago and now her parents are going through the same bruising heartache all over again. Where is God in all this?

There is no issue more challenging to faith than healing. The question of healing cuts to the very heart of faith. Why does God allow suffering? Why did he heal Andrew but not Richard? In continuing to pray for Ann's healing, are we in danger of raising false hopes? Who is to exercise faith – the person who is ill or the person who is praying? And if there is no physical healing, might it be because of a lack of faith?

In this chapter, we will restrict ourselves to a discussion of physical healing. That is not to diminish or devalue other forms of the healing ministry: emotional or inner healing, deliverance from evil spirits and demonic forces, and, most fundamentally, spiritual healing brought about by the forgiveness of sin and reconciliation with God. But it is physical healing that most often challenges our faith.

The problem of suffering

Illness and other forms of suffering bring us face to face with two of the most troubling questions to challenge the Christian faith: Where does suffering come from?

And why does God allow it? There is no complete or easy answer to either, but we can set out biblical principles that point towards some partial answers.

Some accuse God of being the author of suffering. They picture a spiteful God who takes a perverse delight in watching his creatures suffer. To their mind, he is comparable to a miscreant child who pulls the wings off a butterfly, or a cruel adult who puts a kitten in the tumble-dryer. But that is not the Christian God, the God and Father of our Lord Jesus Christ. Our God delights in goodness, not suffering. It was shortly before the onset of Richard's illness that Simon and Eva, our adopted children, moved into our home. Despite the struggle with childlessness, I had come to understand God's goodness at first hand.

When God made the world he made it good, as it repeatedly states in the opening verses of Genesis. Suffering only entered after Adam and Eve, the parents of the human race, took advantage of God's generosity and seized for themselves the one and only thing he had put off-limits – the tree that gave them the knowledge of good and evil. In parallel to this earthly rebellion against the rule and reign of God, it seems there was a heavenly rebellion led by Satan. He was, it appears, originally a privileged and high-ranking angel (see Isaiah 14:12–15; Ezek 28:12b–19 for hints of this) but, following an act of mutiny, he was cast down from heaven to become the Accuser and Tempter of humankind, the one Jesus called 'a liar and a murderer' (John 8:44).

God made the world good. Suffering is an alien intrusion into it. In creation, God brought order out of chaos. Suffering reverses this and brings dis-order and dis-ease to the world and to the lives of those it touches.

Sometimes I meet Christians who blame God for their suffering. But the same people will go to the doctor in the hope of a cure or at least the alleviation of their pain. This is inconsistent. If God wants us to suffer, what are we doing going to the doctor's surgery or the hospital?

God's desire is not that we should suffer, but that we should enjoy good health and a full lifespan. We repeat: *suffering is an alien intrusion into a world that God made good*. Jesus, in his ministry of healing, constantly fought against all forms of suffering. We, through medicine and prayer, are called to do the same.

But even if God is not the author of suffering, if he is an all-powerful God then we have to conclude that, at the very least, he *allows* suffering. This is so, but we should not suppose that he is indifferent or unfeeling towards our suffering. God knows and feels our pain. In his birth and life, Jesus shared our human suffering; through his death and resurrection, he redeemed it. When Richard died, his parents wept; they grieved because they loved their child. But God, who is infinite in love and compassion, loved Richard far more than his deeply devoted parents ever could. When Richard died, I believe Jesus wept for him and his parents, just as he wept for his friend Lazarus when he died (John 11:35). However, there is a difference. When Richard died, his parents grieved for their loss, but Jesus received Richard into his own wonderful presence. For Richard, the suffering was over. God sees things, not least death, from a very different perspective. The diagram opposite may help to explain what I mean.

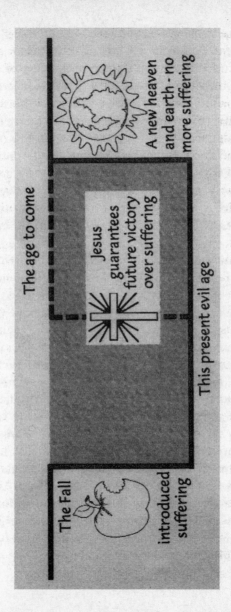

Suffering – an alien intrusion into God's world, which he will one day bring to an end.

God made the world good. Satan's rebellion and humanity's disobedience brought suffering into the world. But one day in the future, because of Christ's victory over all the powers of evil, God will transform and renew our world. There will be a new heaven and a new earth. Creation will no longer be in a state of decay, and there will be 'no more death or mourning or crying or pain' (Rom 8:20–21; Rev 21:4). However, until Christ returns we remain subject to physical decay and death. Disease is an enemy to be aggressively fought against by medicine, by prayer and by maintaining a healthy lifestyle. We will not always win. But full healing, complete wholeness, can only be known in the age to come.

Christians, especially those engaged in the healing ministry, need to come to terms with their mortality. Except for those who will have the privilege of being alive when Christ returns, we will all die one day. No-one dies of nothing. Physical death is the result of the body failing to function in some way. Death, says Paul, is an enemy, and the last enemy to be defeated (1 Cor 15:26). Until it is defeated, we continue to battle against everything which is life-threatening and which causes suffering. The final outcome of this battle is not in doubt, for God is sovereign. But until Christ comes again to claim and proclaim the victory that is already his, suffering will remain, though it will always be limited by God in what it can do (Job 1:12; 2:6) Alongside our present suffering there will be gracious glimpses of the joy and glory to come, including those glimpses resulting from God's wonderful healing power and love breaking through in the here and now.

Does God have a purpose in suffering?

When God does not heal, we naturally search for an explanation. One of the most common is that God may be allowing suffering to continue because he has a purpose in it, a lesson for us to learn. An oft-quoted text to support this view are Paul's words in Romans 8:28: 'We know that in all things God works for the good of those who love him, who have been called according to his purpose.' If we think God has a purpose in suffering, we may hesitate to pray for healing, or we may expend vast amounts of energy struggling to figure out what this purpose is, what lesson we are supposed to be learning.

Just occasionally, suffering does have a purpose. If we pick up a hot dinner plate it will burn our fingers. The pain tells us to put it down quickly before we do any lasting damage to ourselves. We do not mind that kind of pain. Similarly, a series of headaches may indicate we are overworking and need to slow down before something worse happens. But the most serious suffering has no intrinsic value or purpose. Medical textbooks are full of diseases and disorders that are nothing but destructive to the human body and brain. Does Ann's cancer have a purpose? Is that why she has not yet received healing? No, emphatically no! Only a very twisted mind would suggest that there was some purpose or value in a debilitating, life-threatening and cruel disease. Suffering brings disorder and disarray to our lives, not benefit.

However, although suffering has no purpose, because God is sovereign he can work his own purposes

out *through* suffering. Not every experience in life is
good – many are downright evil – but God can turn even
the least desirable of circumstances around for his own
higher purposes. The Old Testament story of Joseph
illustrates this (Gen 37–50). Joseph's brothers sold him
into slavery, telling their father Jacob that he had been
killed by a wild animal. Later, in Egypt, a false accusa-
tion of rape put Joseph in prison for several years. Later
still, because of his gift in interpreting dreams, he was
made minister of state and was able to save Egypt in a
time of famine. When he was finally reunited with his
ill-intentioned brothers, he forgave them. This is what
he told them: 'You intended to harm me, but God
intended it for good to accomplish what is now being
done, the saving of many lives' (50:20).

There was nothing good about Joseph's experiences
– there is nothing good in attempted murder, cruel slavery, false accusations and imprisonment – but God, in
his sovereign power and merciful kindness, was able to
work out his own higher and greater purposes in
Joseph's suffering.

> It is God's nature to heal, not to 'teach' through sickness.
> Sickness is generally not beneficial. If we are drawn
> nearer to God because of sickness, the virtue lies in
> God's goodness which leads us to repentance and
> acceptance, rather than in what the sickness has done.[1]

Paul's thorn in the flesh

Another frequently quoted passage used to bolster the
argument that God might have something to teach
through suffering is 2 Corinthians 12 – the passage

describing Paul's 'thorn in the flesh'. Although many interpreters assume that this thorn was some kind of physical affliction (possibly the eye condition Paul seems to be hinting at in Galatians 4:13–15), this is probably not what Paul means. The expression 'thorn in the flesh' (or something similar) is also found in the Old Testament (Num 33:55; Josh 23:13; Judges 2:3) where it does not refer to physical illness but to military attacks upon Israel by her enemies.

The biblical expression 'thorn in the flesh' is rather like our more modern expression 'pain in the neck'. When we call someone a pain in the neck, we do not mean they are the cause of physical pain, only that they are a tiresome nuisance! This is what Paul seems to be saying about his thorn, which he further identifies as a 'messenger of Satan' (2 Cor 12:7). In chapters 11 and 12 of 2 Corinthians, he discusses his sufferings, which are not physical illness but persecution. He is not boasting or rejoicing in illness but in the privilege of enduring insults, hardships and persecution for the Lord. The most natural conclusion is that Paul's 'thorn in the flesh' was not a physical ailment at all but the constant and severe persecution, orchestrated by Satan, the purpose of which was to undermine his gospel ministry.

Even if Paul's thorn is understood as an illness or physical condition, this passage cannot be used as an excuse for not praying for healing. Whatever the thorn was, Paul prayed more than once for it to be taken away from him. The New Testament nowhere suggests that we passively accept physical illness, let alone rejoice in it or see it as God-sent. Likewise, Jesus never turned away anyone on the grounds that it might be God's will for

them to suffer, or that God might have some lesson for
them to learn from their pain:

> A man with leprosy came and knelt before him and said,
> 'Lord, if you are willing, you can make me clean.'
>   Jesus reached out his hand and touched the man. 'I
> am willing,' he said. 'Be clean!' Immediately he was cured
> of his leprosy.
>
> *(Matthew 8:2–3)*

There is no doubt as to Jesus' willingness to heal this
man. Unhesitatingly he reached out in compassion and,
by his touch, the man was not only healed of his physical ailment but also restored to his place in a society
which had spurned his very existence. He was healed
and made whole.

Sometimes people talk of their suffering as the cross
God has given them to carry. But the only cross Jesus
ever expected his followers to carry was to endure hos-
tility and persecution for the sake of the gospel, never
the suffering that comes with illness (Mark 8:34). Jesus
came to heal, and he commanded his disciples to do the
same (Matt 10:8). To pray against suffering and for healing is never wrong. Although answers are never guaranteed, we can always ask. Our God is a loving heavenly
Father who delights to give good gifts to his children
(7:11), so we need have no doubts about his goodness or
his power.

Sickness and sin

Another reason often put forward for the absence of healing in response to prayer, is sin. The man with leprosy in

the incident above may well have thought that his suffering was a result of sin, either personal sin or sin that had occurred somewhere in his family tree. Might Jesus be unwilling to heal him, he may have thought, because he was suffering the just deserts of this sin? In the Old Testament, Job's three so-called 'comforters' repeatedly made the suggestion that some sin, perhaps long-forgotten, must be the root cause of his suffering (Eliphaz, in Job 22:4–11). But it was not the case. Though no-one is ever sinless, God's verdict on Job was that he was 'blameless and upright, a man who fears God and shuns evil' (1:8; 2:3).

Back in the New Testament, the theory that suffering is caused by sin is again put to the test and found wanting:

> As [Jesus] went along, he saw a man blind from birth. His disciples asked him, 'Rabbi, who sinned, this man or his parents, that he was born blind?'
>
> 'Neither this man nor his parents sinned,' said Jesus, 'but this happened so that the work of God might be displayed in his life.'
>
> *(John 9:1–3)*

The Jewish rabbis of the day held to a maxim: 'There is no death without sin, and there is no suffering without iniquity.' They mistakenly and cruelly taught that if a child was born with a handicap, it must either have been because his parents or grandparents had sinned against God, or because the child had sinned before birth as an embryo in the womb.

This was the teaching upon which the disciples were basing what was to them an obvious and logical question (v 2). Sadly, their interest was prompted more by theological curiosity than compassion. For them the blind man was a riddle to be solved rather than a sufferer to be relieved. But Jesus refused to accept either of the two alternatives set before him by rabbinic teaching. Instead, he looked on the man's plight as an opportunity to show compassion and to do God's work. He is unequivocal in his response: 'Neither this man nor his parents sinned, but this happened so that the work of God might be displayed in his life.'

While it is true that all suffering is an *indirect* result of humanity's rebellion against God, it is certainly not true that the suffering of an individual is always or even mostly a *direct* result of personal sin. 'Although sickness comes ultimately because of the curse of sin, not all sicknesses are caused by specific sins.'[2]

In a small minority of cases, sickness *will* be the result of personal sin. One rather obvious example is sexually-transmitted disease when it is caught by breaking God's laws on sexual behaviour. Other, but less obvious, cases of sin resulting in sickness might be heart disease brought on by overwork, or high blood pressure brought on by being overweight. All these are abuses of our God-given bodies intended to be temples of his Holy Spirit. But even if we can see a link between a person's sickness and a sinful lifestyle, we need to resist being judgemental. Those who have brought suffering upon themselves are usually only too painfully aware of the fact. They need to hear the message of God's love, not his judgement.

Many Christians live unnecessarily under condemnation. They are convinced that God loves everyone but them, that they are not worthy enough to merit God's attention. I know Christians who will happily and regularly pray for the healing of others, but would never ask anyone to lay hands on and pray for them. Sometimes this is pride, but more often it is their sense of unworthiness and lack of certainty about God's goodness in general and his love for them in particular. Such people need to be surrounded by love and encouraged to reach out in faith.

The story of the blind man in John chapter 9 teaches us another important point: in looking to God for healing, we can be certain that he wants to work for our good, but we can be even more sure that he will work for his own glory (v 3). In John's Gospel especially, Jesus' miracles are often called 'signs'. For example, when he turned water into wine, John comments: 'This, the first of his miraculous signs, Jesus performed at Cana in Galilee. He thus revealed his glory, and his disciples put their faith in him' (2:11). Similarly, when Jesus heard that his friend Lazarus was seriously ill, he said, 'This sickness will not end in death. No, it is for God's glory, so that God's Son may be glorified through it' (11:4). As before, this is not to imply that there is any intrinsic goodness in suffering, only that God is able to take what is evil, overrule it and employ it for his own higher and greater purposes – namely, our good and his glory. However, though sometimes his glory will come through healing, sometimes it will come through the absence of healing. Anyone acquainted with the powerful testimony of Joni Eareckson-Tada cannot doubt this. As a teenager, Joni suffered a terrible diving accident which left her a paraplegic. She is still paralysed, but her ministry has touched the lives of thousands.

Let's summarise where we have got to:

* In his goodness, God's desire is for our health and well-being (see Exod 15:26). He also seeks to bring glory and honour to his own name.

* Suffering is an alien intrusion into a world that God made good. We should see it as such and take a stand against suffering by every means at our disposal.

* While God, in his mercy, may heal here and now (through either medicine, miracles or the body's wonderful powers of natural recovery), suffering will be eradicated only in heaven (Rev 21:4). Only then will we experience full healing in body, mind and spirit.

* Death, the 'last enemy' (1 Cor 15:26), is unavoidable (Job 30:23; Psalm 89:48; Heb 9:27) and we all have to die of something. But death need hold no fear for the Christian (1 Cor 15:53–57; Phil 1:21–23). It is, as the hymn says, 'but the gate of life immortal'.

* Until Christ returns, suffering and death remain in our world, and we are to fight against them. Wholeness can include healing but is always something more than healing.

Healing, faith and common sense

There is a great deal of confusion among Christians

when it comes to the relationship between healing, f......
and common sense, and much misery has been caused
by this confusion.

> Is any one of you in trouble? He should pray. Is anyone
> happy? Let him sing songs of praise. Is any one of you
> sick? He should call the elders of the church to pray
> over him and anoint him with oil in the name of the
> Lord. And the prayer offered in faith will make the sick
> person well; the Lord will raise him up. If he has sinned,
> he will be forgiven. Therefore confess your sins to each
> other and pray for each other so that you may be
> healed. The prayer of a righteous man is powerful and
> effective.
>
> *(James 5:13–16)*

As we can see from this passage from James, we should
pray for ourselves and for one another. Church leaders
have a particular responsibility to pray for the sick; the
assumption here seems to be that they are the ones who
will exercise faith. Faith, as we have seen, is a blend of
expectancy and obedience. Sometimes there will be
great expectancy but no healing. At other times,
expectancy may be almost negligible (as was the case
when I prayed with Andrew), but there will be healing
nevertheless. But more important than expectancy is
obedience. Of course, if we expect absolutely nothing,
we will not pray at all. But even if there is only very little expectancy – faith the size of a grain of mustard seed
(Matt 17:20) – it is enough. We do not need great faith
in God, but faith in a great God.

But before looking more closely at faith, first a word
about common sense. Faith does not work in opposition
to common sense. Praise God for modern medicine!

Alongside prayer for illness, I would always urge someone to seek the best medical help available for their particular complaint. I would also urge those who believe
they have been healed by God always to go back to their
doctor before discontinuing any prescribed medical
treatment.

When, if ever, might common sense suggest that we
should not pray for healing? Broadly speaking, there are
two occasions when I don't. First, when there is
advanced terminal illness and the person concerned
would rather seek a quiet end than fight on. Second,
when it is clear that an old person has reached the natural end of a full life and healing would not much
improve the quality of that life. In these two cases, however, I would always want to pray for the relief of pain
and anxiety and, if the person is not a believer, that they
might respond to the love of God in their final days.

Faith is not about psyching ourselves up, or closing
our eyes to the reality of our situation, gritting our teeth
and believing the seemingly impossible for all we are
worth. Faith is not an attempt to exercise mind over
matter or bend God to do our will. Faith is about knowing what God *can* do and then being obedient and
receptive to what God *might* do.

Sometimes we will come to God more out of desperation than expectancy. In my church in Sheffield, we
used to invite people to come forward to the commun-
ion rail to receive prayer for healing. On occasions too
numerous to count, the person coming forward would
tell me their need, but then go on to explain they did not
have much faith. I would point out to them that they
had in fact made the decision to leave their pew, come

forward and ask for prayer. That, I told them, was an expression of the mustard-seed faith that was pleasing to God.

Looking back to the passage quoted earlier from James, we can see that obedient faith is to be exercised both by those who pray and by those who ask. Those praying are responding obediently and lovingly to the request to come and pray. By being obedient in this way, they are exercising faith. Likewise, the person who is sick is exercising faith by calling for the church and pastoral leaders to come and pray. The sick person may not *feel* as though they have much faith – their request may be born more out of desperation than expectancy – but, nevertheless, they are exercising faith by asking for prayer. Faith, like love, is always a matter of the will rather than of feelings.

Clearly, there is a connection between faith and healing, but it is not easy to define. It is, I believe, entirely wrong and pastorally very damaging to suggest to people that they have not been healed because of their lack of faith. To make such a suggestion adds insult to injury. Not infrequently Jesus said to individuals, 'Your faith has made you well', but he never did the opposite. He never rebuked a sick or needy person for a lack of faith in the way that he sometimes rebuked his disciples for being 'of little faith' as, for example, when they thought they were all going to drown (Matt 8:26), when Peter began to sink (14:31), or when nine out of the twelve failed to drive a demon out of a man's son (17:20).

In the Gospels, more inhibiting than a lack of faith on the part of the sick individual seems to be the absence of faith in the general environment. In

Nazareth, Jesus' home town, even he 'did not do many miracles there because of their lack of faith' (Matt 13:58). The report in Mark's Gospel is more expansive: 'Jesus could not do any miracles there, except lay his hands on a few sick people and heal them. And he was amazed at their lack of faith' (Mark 6:5–6). This is in contrast to other occasions when he healed all who came to him (Matt 4:24, 8:16, 9:35, 12:15, 14:36).

Personally, there are times when I would be more than happy to settle for the healing of 'a few sick people'. As I write, we have not only Ann, whom I have already mentioned, but several others in our church for whom we are praying. A young husband and father with multiple sclerosis. Another man with near-daily head pains that have cut short his working life. And my own wife, Sarah, who has a depressive disorder which means frequent and prolonged stays in hospital. I long for God to break in! And then there are the countless others outside our churches whose lives are diminished and impoverished through pain and suffering. We do not know their names, but God knows each one by name and cares for them just as much as he cares for Andrew, Richard, Ann and Sarah.

I am increasingly convinced that one reason why we see so few miracles of healing is the general lack of faith that pervades the church in Western society today. In other parts of the world, in churches we would perhaps regard as less sophisticated, Christians are seeing quite extraordinary demonstrations of God's healing power. In the West, however, we have bishops and theologians who have so completely imbibed a rationalistic worldview that not only do they deny the possibility of modern miracles, they dismiss the biblical record, refusing to take at face value events like the crossing of the Red Sea, the virgin birth of Christ and even his resurrection. And those of us who believe our Bibles do not act upon what those Bibles tell us: we hide in our churches when we should be taking the signs of God's love into a broken world. God have mercy on us.

The frustrating lack of healing that we see in our churches is indeed a challenge to faith, but we can respond in one of two ways. We can rewrite our Bibles, give up and think that there is no point in praying; or we can fight on in the battle against suffering in all its forms and thereby play our part in answering the prayer that Jesus taught us: 'your kingdom come, your will be done on earth as it is in heaven' (Matt 6:10). In his sermon on the mount, Jesus said, 'Seek first his kingdom and his righteousness ... Ask and it will be given to you; seek and you will find; knock and the door will be opened to you. For everyone who asks receives; he who seeks finds; and to him who knocks, the door will be opened' (6:33; 7:7–8). Similarly, his parable of the persistent widow (Luke 18:1–8) encourages us to be insistent and specific, not vague and wishy-washy, in our praying. God is our loving heavenly Father who delights to give good gifts to his children (Luke 11:11–13).

Children in their simplicity ask for precisely what they want. If a child wants a bicycle she will ask for a bicycle; and she will probably know the make and colour she wants too. It is only adults who drop silly hints, saying things like 'I'd like a surprise', when what they really want is the latest blockbuster from their favourite

author. When we are sick, we can ask God for healing
without trying to double-guess what he is thinking,
whether it is his will to heal or not, whether there is
some hidden sin we need to remedy first, whether he
wants us to learn this or that lesson in our suffering.

The past twenty-five to thirty years have seen a
renewed commitment to the healing ministry of the
church. It is a ministry that calls for obedient faith and
enduring faithfulness. It calls for a compassionate faith
which takes the risk of getting involved with suffering
and hurting people. It calls for a wise and discerning
faith which rejoices at every evidence of God's love. And
it calls for a loving and sensitive faith which stands by
the sick whether their healing is to be in this lifetime or
the life to come. It calls for down-to-earth, common-
sense pastoral care.

We still have much to learn, and as yet our collective
faith may be not much bigger than a mustard seed. But
it is a start.

∞ Notes

1. John Wimber, Healing Seminar 1, Vineyard
   Ministries International, 1984, p 13.

2. Wimber, Seminar 1, p 13.

∞ Further reading

Francis McNutt, *Healing*, Ave Maria Press, 1974.
McNutt, *The Power to Heal*, Ave Maria Press, 1977.
John Wimber & Kevin Springer, *Power Healing*,
     Hodder and Stoughton, 1986.

Jim Glennon, *Your Healing is Within You*, Hodder and
  Stoughton, 1978.
Joni Eareckson–Tada, *The Joni Story*, Marshall
  Pickering, 1996.
Mark Pearson, *Christian Healing*, Hodder and
  Stoughton, 1996.

✆ Questions to think about

1. Have you, or anyone close to you, ever been healed
   in answer to prayer? How did you feel about it?

2. Have you ever known anyone who has not been
   healed despite much prayer and apparent faith?
   How did they handle it? And how did you feel
   about it?

3. Where do you think death fits into God's scheme of
   life? How do you feel about old age and your own
   mortality?

4. How do you view suffering? Where do you think it
   comes from?

5. What, if anything, makes you hesitant about
   praying for healing?

6. How do faith and common sense fit together in
   praying for healing?

Chapter Six

THE GIFTS AND GUIDANCE OF THE SPIRIT

We were coming to the end of our evening service. A thought formed in my head. I did not hear any words or see any pictures – it was simply a fleeting impression, but one which I sensed came from outside, not inside. I put the thought into words: 'I believe there may be someone present who thinks she is pregnant, isn't sure, but certainly doesn't want to be.' As a quick after-thought born out of simple pastoral common sense, I added that if anyone did respond to this 'word', she would be guaranteed confidentiality and sensitivity.

At the end of the service we offered prayer for anyone who might want to receive ministry. A number came, including one young lady who was eager to tell me she was not coming in response to my 'word' but for some-thing completely different! After perhaps twenty min-utes, those who had come for prayer had been attended to. Both pray-ees and pray-ers began to drift away. But still no–one had responded to my 'word'. Had I misheard God, or didn't the person concerned feel able to respond?

I went to pick up my preaching notes and turned for the door. It was then I saw Rachel (not her real name) sitting quietly on a seat in the front row. I went over, sat down next to her and, in the now almost empty church, listened to her story.

Rachel had taken a gap-year between school and university. In that year she had gone to Africa to do voluntary Christian work. Her home church was very proud and supportive of her, and had looked upon her as 'their missionary'. During the year she befriended an emotionally needy young man in the country in which she was working. One thing led to another and they formed a sexual relationship just before she left to come home. To have told her parents or her church any of this would have been painfully difficult, so Rachel's guilty secret was also a lonely one. Now, in her first few weeks at university, in unfamiliar surroundings, the signs were that she was pregnant.

What followed next was a matter of offering the appropriate pastoral and practical care through which Rachel was reassured of God's love. It turned out that she *was* pregnant. Common sense took over. Her parents were contacted – they proved to be far more understanding than she ever expected. Her church was supportive too. Rachel left university and moved into a flat near home. Just before she left, she came to see me once more. She explained that my 'word of knowledge' (as this particular gift of the Spirit is usually identified) had come at just the right time. A week or two earlier and she would not have been worrying; a week or two later and she would have been panicking. The guilt of her sexual relationship had blighted her relationship with God. The word of knowledge and its perfect timing had reassured her of God's love, and she had found his forgiveness.

Words of knowledge and healing are just two of th[e] nine 'gifts of the Spirit' listed in 1 Corinthians chapter 12. This list is not exhaustive – there are others that are not included, for example, the pictures and visions we frequently encounter in the book of Acts and in the Old Testament.

The rediscovery of the gifts of the Spirit by churches within the mainline denominations has been both welcome and divisive. Churches have split over the issue, and ministers have resigned their pastorates. I have pastored churches in which the gifts of the Spirit have been a regular and accepted part of worship; and I have led other churches which would feel very uncomfortable if someone spoke in tongues, gave a word or reported a picture they had seen. A variety of theological positions is used to justify each type of response, but in reality the reaction is more likely to be an emotional rather than a theological one. So let's start with the evidence of scripture.

There are three lists of gifts to be found in the New Testament: the gifts of the Spirit in 1 Corinthians 12:4–11,27–31; the gifts of servant leadership (apostle, prophet, evangelist, pastor and teacher) in Ephesians 4:11–13; and a more general list in Romans 12:4–8 (prophecy, serving, teaching, encouraging, contributing to the needs of others, leadership and showing mercy). Christian writers and preachers commonly amalgamate all these lists into one, and then invite people to suggest what they think their particular gift may be. Invariably, more 'spiritual' types home in on the supernatural gifts while more 'practical' church members identify gifts such as serving, administration or encouraging others.

There is some justification for doing this – giving out

the hymn books with a cheery smile is as important to the Lord as giving an earth-stopping word of prophecy – but such an approach fails to distinguish between those gifts which are *supernatural* in origin and those which are *natural*, albeit enriched and enhanced by the Holy Spirit's energies. Amalgamating the gifts into one super-list also fails to take into account the context of the three different passages: Ephesians chapter 4 lists gifts given *by Christ* for church leadership; Romans chapter 12 lists gifts given *by God* for sacrificial Christian service of the kind to be undertaken by all church members; and 1 Corinthians chapter 12 lists gifts given *by the Spirit* when the church comes together for worship.

While in no way deprecating or devaluing the gifts found in the first two lists, we will focus our attention upon the gifts of the Spirit itemised in 1 Corinthians chapter 12 and further discussed in chapter 14 of the same epistle. To discuss each gift in detail is beyond the scope of this book, but we can set out a brief definition and an example of each in tabular form:

Gift	Definition	Example
Wisdom	An insightful answer to a challenging question, usually while evangelising.	John 4: Jesus' answer to the Samaritan woman about the right place to worship.
Knowledge	Knowing a fact about a person or problem that only God could have revealed.	Jesus' knowledge of the Samaritan woman's five previous husbands.

Gift	Definition	Example
Faith	Not saving faith, but a certainty about something God is intending to do.	Acts 27: Paul's certainty that he and his shipmates would be safe in the storm.
Healing	The healing of someone who is sick in body, mind or spirit.	Acts 28: Paul's prayer for the father of the Maltese governor.
Miracles	Extraordinary and immediate healing or a display of God's power over nature.	1 Kings 18: Elijah calling fire down from heaven.
Prophecy	Bringing a God-given message for an individual or group. A prophecy does not necessarily predict the future, but more often brings a present challenge.	All the Old Testament prophets. Agabus, in Acts 11:27–28 and 21:10–11; although his prophecies were accurate, Paul chose not to take his advice!
Discernment	The testing of the origin of a spirit or message: Is it from God or not?	Acts 16:16–18: The fortune-telling girl in Philippi, who followed Paul around.

Gift	Definition	Example
Tongues	Speaking to God in an unknown language of praise or prayer.	Acts 2:4,7–11; 10:46; 19:6.
Interpretation	The interpretation of a tongue when an individual uses the latter in worship. A tongue and its interpretation should not be equated with a prophecy.	1 Cor 14:5,26–28.

Range of views

There is a wide range of views and attitudes towards the gifts of the Spirit. A few conservative Christians still argue that the gifts ceased soon after the apostolic era. Such a view is not tenable. Whatever one makes of the Pentecostal and charismatic movements of the twentieth century, the experience of Christians in such churches is clear testimony to the fact that the gifts of the Spirit have not been withdrawn. The truth is that the gifts of the Spirit *are* available today. (Those who argue that the gifts of the Spirit have died out, usually do so from a misinterpretation of 1 Corinthians 13:8–10 which says that the gifts of the Spirit will cease 'when perfection comes'. But perfection will be when we see God 'face to face' (v 12), at the second coming of Christ, and not before.)

A more common view is that such 'primitive' manifestations of the Spirit are no longer really necessary now that the church has matured and has the New Testament scriptures and scholarly resources so readily available. Those who take this line are quick to warn against dependence on subjective, emotional experiences rather than the objective truth of God's Word. But, as we shall see, the gifts of the Spirit need not be dependent on an emotionally-charged atmosphere. And, while it is true that we have the New Testament available to study at our leisure and two thousand years of church history and scholarship beneath our belts, I remain to be convinced that we are any more mature in Christ or stronger in faith than the early church!

Others are simply uncomfortable with the gifts of the Spirit. They may feel that charismatic worship is in danger of getting out of control, or they may have had a bad experience – being made to feel like second-class Christians because they do not speak in tongues or have a particular gift. Still others are suspicious of the gifts of the Spirit because they have only ever met examples that seem to trivialise the whole affair: nothing but pictures of doves flying in and out through church windows, rivers watering the desert, prophecies beginning 'I am your children and I love you', or words of knowledge given in a congregation of several hundred when it is a safe bet, for example, that 'there is someone here with a headache'!

Those who belong to churches where the gifts of the Spirit are an accepted and regular part of worship believe that supernatural phenomena, including tongues and prophecy, should be happening all the time. They rejoice not only in the manifestation of these gifts, but also in such things as the 'signs and wonders' ministry of the late John Wimber, the Toronto Blessing (in which people fall to the ground, laugh and cry) and, more recently, the Pensacola experience. Such phenomena are taken as evidence of God's blessing. The unspoken implication is this: 'They are happening in my church. If they are not happening in yours, then there is something wrong with your faith!'

New Testament worship

It is a curious thing, but nowhere in the New Testament do we find a complete description of early Christian worship. The nearest thing to a church service is found in Acts 20:7–12, where we have an account of Paul's stay at Troas – the occasion when a young worshipper fell asleep during the sermon while sitting on a third-storey window sill! If we were to try to copy this example in a literal way, we would have services that went on through the night, very lengthy sermons and bars at the windows to prevent accidents! Lacking a clear blueprint of worship, we must conclude that God has given us remarkable freedom when it comes to styles and forms of worship. But within that worship, what part are the gifts of the Spirit to play? Only three things can be said with any certainty:

• *The gifts of the Spirit are a part of worship, but not the central part*

Paul only draws attention to the gifts of the Spirit when

things go wrong, as they did in Corinth. The church members there were misusing the gifts of the Spirit, employing them to show their spiritual prowess in front of others. The gifts are not for inflating egos or demolishing others, but for building up the whole church and strengthening it for ministry and mission. Exercising love is more important than exercising gifts of the Spirit (1 Cor 13:1) though, of course, there is no reason why the two should be incompatible.

A summary of Christian worship is given in Acts 2:42. The believers met for teaching, fellowship, the breaking of bread and prayer. Gifts are not mentioned.

• *The gifts of the Spirit were shared by the congregation, not just the leaders*

> When you come together, everyone has a hymn, or a word of instruction, a revelation, a tongue or an interpretation. All of these must be done for the strengthening of the church.
>
> *(1 Corinthians 14:26)*

This verse gives a very different picture of worship from the one-man band style of worship that takes place in most churches while the congregation remains fixed in their pews. Despite what one might think, Paul's advice is not a recipe for a cacophony but, rather, a beautiful concert, as long as everyone present is prepared to submit to the Holy Spirit as conductor, and those who have come with something to contribute wait their turn and allow their contribution to be evaluated by others (1 Cor 14:26–33).

• *The gifts of the Spirit need not be emotionally charged*

The New English Bible unhelpfully translates the gifts
of tongues as 'ecstatic utterances' or 'tongues (or language) of ecstasy', suggesting that those using the gift
have somehow lost control of at least a part of themselves. This is not the case. A person worshipping in
tongues may be caught up in a flow of wonder, love and
praise to God, just as she might in her own native language, but she still has full control of her vocal faculties.
The Holy Spirit does not take control of a person in a
way that an evil spirit attempts to do. He is a Spirit of
liberty.

There is no reason why charismatic worship need
get out of hand:

> The spirits of prophets are subject to the control of
> prophets. For God is not a God of disorder but of
> peace. ...
>   Be eager to prophesy, and do not forbid speaking in
> tongues. But everything should be done in a fitting and
> orderly way.
>
> (1 Cor 14:32–33,39–40).

Jackie Pullinger, when she first went to minister to the
drug addicts and triad gangs of Hong Kong's once infa-
mous Walled City, describes how she set about praying
in tongues each day for fifteen minutes 'by the clock'.
There was nothing ecstatic about her experience;
instead it felt almost boring. But what it did lead to was
a wonderful evangelistic breakthrough in her work
which, until then, seemed to be getting nowhere.

• Spiritual gifts used in the New Testament church

Chapters 13 and 15 of the book of Acts give us clues as to the relative importance of the gifts of the Spirit within the early church. Acts chapter 13 begins:

> In the church at Antioch there were prophets and teachers: Barnabas, Simeon called Niger, Lucius of Cyrene, Manaen (who had been brought up with Herod the tetrarch) and Saul. While they were worshipping the Lord and fasting, the Holy Spirit said, 'Set apart for me Barnabas and Saul for the work to which I have called them.' So after they had fasted and prayed, they placed their hands on them and sent them off.

The chapter goes on to describe the start of Paul's first missionary journey.

The gift of prophecy, calling for Paul (then named Saul) and Barnabas to be set aside for this task, was given to an outward-looking, mission-orientated church. They were not seeking God's blessing for themselves but for the world around them. One of my concerns today is that churches are seeking spiritual phenomena (especially the Toronto Blessing and its like) in a selfish way, to help them feel better about themselves rather than engage with a suffering world. Talk of 'waves of the Spirit' makes me fearful that churches are chasing the latest fad without exercising due discernment. (For more on this, read *Charismatic Renewal* by Tom Smail, Andrew Walker and Nigel Wright.)

There are a few other things to note, too. First, the response to the prophecy was not immediate. There was further prayer and fasting before Paul and Barnabas were commissioned and sent off. This gave time for the prophecy to be weighed. Second, as well as the prophets, there were teachers present who could apply their knowledge of scripture. (Apostles, teachers and prophets are mentioned together as church leaders in various parts of the New Testament, eg 1 Cor 12:28–29; Eph 4:11.)

Third, notice that we are not told the name of the person who gave the prophecy. It may have been one of the leaders named alongside Paul and Barnabas – Simeon, Lucius or Manaen – or it may have been some-body completely different. But the important thing is, he did not get the attention or the praise. The focus of attention was not the individual through whom the message came but the mission to which God was calling the church. Similarly, in the Old Testament, a prophet would often be referred to simply as 'the man of God': his name was not given and he was happy to remain anonymous. Humility, not pride, is called for in the exercise of the gifts.

In Acts chapter 13, we see how a gift of the Spirit was employed in the guidance of the church; but in Acts chapter 15, guidance comes through very different means. At the end of their missionary journey, Paul and Barnabas were asked to file a report with the apostles and elders of the church in Jerusalem. A difficult decision had to be made. Should the newly converted Gentile Christians be expected to undergo circumcision and accept the law of Moses as the Jewish Christians did?

The debate that followed only reached a conclusion after James had made a common-sense proposal, one that he supported with words from the Old Testament prophet Amos (9:11–12). No gift of the Spirit is involved (except perhaps the gift of wisdom), no message in prophecy or tongues, no vision or picture; just logical, common-sense argument conducted in an atmosphere of frank honesty, mutual respect and submission to the Holy Spirit. The decision – not to burden the Gentiles with circumcision or anything else, apart from a few simple requirements – was conveyed with the following words: 'It seemed good to the Holy Spirit and to us' (Acts 15:28).

The decision made in Acts chapter 13 as a consequence of prophecy was no better or more important than the one made in Acts chapter 15 as a result of debate, common sense and the application of scripture. Both were important, both were 'spiritual', both were the result of the activity of God's Spirit – the one through direct supernatural methods, the other through indirect natural means.

Before we leave Acts chapters 13 and 15, it is worth reiterating the point I made earlier in chapter four. The supernatural is not un-natural or anti-natural, yet we so easily drive a wedge between the natural and supernatural, which does not exist in scripture. In Acts chapter 13, the prophecy was discussed before being acted upon. There was common sense as well as faith. And in Acts chapter 15, James' common-sense approach was marked as much by its spiritual wisdom as by its logic: he had the mind of Christ on this matter. For the Jewish Christians to welcome converted Gentiles on equal terms was, in fact, a huge step of faith, requiring them to put aside many of their most treasured religious principles and practices. The church had been prepared for this step by Peter's vision at Joppa (Acts 10).

Faith and common sense

But what of faith and common sense? I want to make a plea, or a series of pleas.

• *To the non-charismatic, and those suspicious of the gifts of the Spirit*

Have more faith and be biblical. Though perhaps not central or essential to Christian worship, the gifts of the Spirit are gifts that God wants the church to use. We are the poorer without them.

That thought or impression which flashed through your mind during worship; that inner prompting to share a verse of scripture with the anxious-looking young person in the pew in front; the conviction you sensed at a church meeting that the proposed church extension should be double- not single-storeyed, even if it is not yet clear where the money might come from for such a venture of faith – all these may well be from God. A word of prophecy does not have to be dressed up in spiritual language or 'King James Version' English. 'I think the Lord may be guiding us to start a lunch club for the older folk' is no different from 'Thus saith the Lord: I am sending you to wait upon the tables of the grey-haired and bald-headed'! And the former may be a good deal easier to understand and less intimidating for others to evaluate.

A stepping-out in faith is necessary if we are to grow in the gifts of the Spirit, but it need not be such a big step. The step of faith I took in giving that word of knowledge about Rachel was not really so great. Might I have looked a bit of an idiot if there had been no response? Perhaps. But the church is family, and it would not have mattered that much. Unless the gifts of the Spirit are abused by the power-happy and pastorally insensitive, there is no reason why mistakes should lead to any damage. A loving fellowship, with trustworthy and sensitive leaders and an atmosphere conducive to the gifts, is the right environment and a safe one in which to discover and explore the gifts God has for his people. (A home or cell group may be a better place to begin this process of discovery than a Sunday service.)

No one walks before they can run. The gifts of the Spirit are something in which individuals and churches grow. Mistakes will be made, excesses may need to be corrected, but far too many Christians have already 'thrown the baby out with the bath water' in this matter.

• To the charismatic and those who rejoice in the gifts of the Spirit

Have more common sense and, again, be biblical. Don't imagine that the word which comes through supernatural means is better than the word which comes through other means. Don't think that a service of worship in which the gifts of the Spirit are evident is more blessed than one in which they are not. Use the gifts God gives, but use them to encourage or build up, not to parade your or your church's spiritual credentials.

I would also ask you to re-evaluate such phenomena as those coming from Toronto and Pensacola. Where in scripture do we see such phenomena? What is their lasting value? Do they encourage churches simply to feel better about themselves, or are they being empowered to go out in mission? What are you more hungry for – the spiritual blessing, or the God who gives it?

• To both sides

To both charismatic and non-charismatic alike, I would
make a plea for greater unity and understanding. There
are clear signs that evangelicals who once stuck together for mutual support are now subdividing into various
camps and tribes which have less and less to do with one
another. Spring Harvest, perhaps the most visible
expression of the strength of British evangelicalism,
already offers holiday weeks with different 'flavours' to
cater, on the one hand, for those who want an emphasis
on 'the Word' and, on the other, for those who want an
emphasis on 'the Spirit'. The creation of such camps
and groupings is to the detriment of all, for we have
much to learn from one another. More importantly, it is
to the detriment of our common gospel mission. For
many outside, the disunity of the church is a barrier to
belief. Jesus prayed that his followers might 'be one ...
that the world may believe' (John 17:21).

Although I want to take the Bible seriously and
believe spiritual gifts should be one part of our worship
today, there is a part of me that could happily live without them. Sometimes, when I see the divisiveness and
pastoral problems they bring, I find myself wondering if
the benefit they offer is worth all the aggro that often
accompanies them. But cynicism is an unhealthy attitude. We should not quench the Spirit, despise prophecies or forbid speaking in tongues (1 Thess 5:19–20; 1
Cor 14:39). Indeed, in the spirit of love, we must 'eager-
ly desire spiritual gifts, especially the gift of prophecy'
(1 Cor 14:1). With unity and understanding, with faith
and common sense, we need to grow in maturity. This
does not mean settling for a quiet life or 'going soft' (as

some mature people do around the middle), nor does it mean a loss of spiritual appetite or zeal.

When the Israelites were crossing the desert, two men, Eldad and Medad, began prophesying publicly:

> …the Spirit also rested on them, and they prophesied in the camp. A young man ran and told Moses, 'Eldad and Medad are prophesying in the camp.'
>
> Joshua son of Nun, who had been Moses' assistant since youth, spoke up and said, 'Moses, my lord, stop them!'
>
> But Moses replied, 'I wish that all the LORD's people were prophets and that the LORD would put his Spirit on them!
>
> *(Numbers 11:26–29)*

Perhaps, as we recover the gifts of the Spirit, we will have to put up with very generalised and predictable messages of doves, rivers and waterfalls – spiritual gifting, like much else, involves a learning process. But we should pray especially for prophets, and for prophecies, which stand out from the crowd, which address the deepest needs of church and nation, which point to ways towards mission, evangelism and social justice that enable the Christian community to have a truly effective impact on our society as we enter the third millennium.

Today, we need men and women of God who are happy to take no glory for themselves, who are not bothered about the labels – flattering or cynical – given them by their fellow Christians, and who, with imagination and courage, bring God's contemporary word to both church and society. They will be people who wrestle in prayer, who can hold a Bible in one hand and a newspaper in the other, who can discern the mind of

Christ and read the signs of the times. And they will be people who are faithful at all times to exercise bold, audacious faith when it matters most.

✆ For further reading

Tom Smail, Andrew Walker & Nigel Wright,
    Charismatic Renewal, SPCK, 1995.
Geoffrey Lay, *Seeking Signs and Missing Wonders*,
    Monarch, 1998.
Michael Green, *I Believe in the Holy Spirit*, Hodder
    and Stoughton, 1985.
D Bridge & D Phypers, *Spiritual Gifts and the Church*,
    Christian Focus, 1995.

✆ Questions to think about

1. What is your experience of the supernatural gifts of the Spirit? Do you think your experience, good or bad, has coloured the way you think about spiritual gifts?

2. How do you feel about the attitude to the gifts of the Spirit adopted by the church where you worship?

3. Have you ever been aware of God prompting you to give a message or offer a picture, which you have not acted upon? What would help you to step out in faith?

4. How do you think the gifts of the Spirit should be tested? Against the Bible? Against common sense?

Chapter Seven

FAITH AT WORK

Susan, a rather attractive girl as I remember, attended the same youth group to which I once belonged. She also had a part-time job in a local shoe shop. She was shy but eager to witness for the Lord. She found a way of doing this by slipping a tract into every pair of shoes sold. One day the manager found out and that was that: she got the sack.

She went up in the estimation of the youth group and in mine (though that was as much because of her good looks as any evangelistic gifts she possessed), but what she had done also raised questions. Was it right for a Christian to witness in such a way? Wasn't this a breach of the trust the shop put in its staff, who were there to represent the store and not the Lord Jesus? Was it the best – or only – way to witness at work? And in any case, does the significance of our working lives consist solely in the number of people to whom we manage to witness? What value – apart from witnessing to colleagues and customers and earning a living – should a Christian attach to secular work?

As a pastor I have observed that church members

struggle over the area of work more than almost any other aspect of their lives. How does faith relate to work? Is it simply a matter of toiling conscientiously and honestly, steering clear of the office gossip and wearing a fish lapel badge in the hope (or perhaps fear) that during the tea break someone might ask what it stands for?

Mark Greene, in his highly commendable book, *Thank God it's Monday*, offers some revealing statistics.[1] According to his research, more than fifty per cent of Christians have never heard a single sermon on the subject of work, while fewer than twenty-five per cent have ever been asked by their minister about their witness while at work. Yet many of us spend up to half our waking hours at work – and I happily include in that figure those whose full-time work is looking after the home and family.

Many Christians see work as a necessary evil, the purpose of which is to earn a crust, afford some evangelistic opportunities and generally fill the time between weekends. On more occasions than I care to remember, I have overheard church members talk about 'getting topped up' on Sundays so that they can somehow survive the week in the world 'out there'. Of course we need spiritual food and refreshment, but the way some Christians speak it's as though they believe God is with them only on Sundays and then abandons them for the rest of the week. However, if God is all-present and all-powerful, as indeed he is, then surely he is with us just as much on a Monday morning in the workplace as he is on a Sunday morning in church. This must be the inevitable conclusion of a proper understanding of the 'otherness' and 'nearness' of God we were looking at in chapter three. And while the world 'out there' can sometimes be hostile to the Christian believer, it is also the world that God made, loves, inhabits by his Spirit and seeks to redeem through the presence and activity of his people whom he calls to be its salt and light (Matt 5:13–16).

Creation

To understand the biblical perspective on work, we must begin with creation. In the opening two chapters of the Bible, we discover that God is a worker. Creation is his work. Designing and building the universe from scratch isn't bad for a week's effort in a new job! Our God is a creative God, and he invites us to join him in fulfilling his purposes for creation.

Work has two principal functions:

- To provide for our needs and those of our fellow human beings;

- To bring order to a disorderly world.

In each of these functions we are copying and building upon the work of God. In creation God has provided for all our needs; in our work we take the raw materials he gives us and use them to supply our needs and those of our neighbour. In creation God brought order out of chaos; in our work we are likewise striving to make the world a more orderly place, one that is better organised, better informed and better equipped to serve human need.

In our work God calls us alongside himself to be his co-creators and co-rulers of the world. We can either abuse this privilege, or use it to his glory and our happiness. The idea that, in our daily occupations, we share in God's work of ordering the world according to his will is one that is absent from other ancient Near Eastern civilisations. In the creation stories that circulated among Israel's ancient neighbours, people were not seen as co-workers with God, but as slaves who worked for the gods while they put up their feet. The work undertaken by human beings was seen not as something creative and pleasurable but as burdensome drudgery.

God took pleasure in his work of creation. At the end of each working day, he was able to look at what he had accomplished and declare it to be good (Gen 1:4,10,12,18,21,25). It seems that even the angels shared in God's joy at the delight of his unfolding creation (Job 38:7). And, at the end of the sixth day, after the creation of humankind in his own image, God was able to look back over his week's work and declare it to be '*very* good' (Gen 1:31). Today, our seven-day week is still defined by God's plan in creation. But even this most basic of principles, with the erosion of Sunday as a special day, is under threat.

It is in his *good* work that God invites us to share as his co-workers. When God put Adam and Eve in Eden, he set them to work: 'The Lord God took the man and put him in the Garden of Eden to work it and take care of it' (Gen 2:15). Adam's reward would be the food he could grow. Eve was created to be his helper (v 18, and notice that here 'helper' means co-worker and companion, not slave or servant).

How wonderful it would be if we could all go home on a Friday evening feeling that we had achieved all we had wanted to achieve during the week; that our time had been used purposefully, productively and with worthwhile results; that it was all 'very good'. The Bible frequently presents work as blessed by God and therefore something enjoyable, creative and productive (Deut 2:7; 14:29; 16:15; 30:9; Job 1:10; Prov 12:14). But this is not our usual experience. We will, more often than not, come home on a Friday feeling exhausted, frustrated and thinking that much of our effort has been wasted. Work can be a curse as well as a blessing. And because of his rebellion, work certainly became more of a chore and less of a joy for Adam:

> To Adam [God] said, ...
> 'Cursed is the ground because of you;
>   through painful toil you will eat of it
>   all the days of your life.
> It will produce thorns and thistles for you,
>   and you will eat the plants of the field.
> By the sweat of your brow
>   you will eat your food
> until you return to the ground,
>   since from it you were taken...'
>
> *(Genesis 3:17–19)*

In other words, humankind would have to put more in while getting less back. The world God had made would no longer be so co-operative with humanity's efforts to order it in such a way as to make it fruitful and productive. Extracting a living from creation would be more demanding and back-breaking. It is not surprising then that we find it so difficult to get out of bed on Monday mornings!

Unless the Lord builds the house,
      its builders labour in vain.

                                        (Psalm 127:1)

When they are in opposition to God, human achievement and technology are destructive of human relationships and lead to the harmful competitive spirit characteristic of so many working environments today. The story of the tower of Babel is representative of humankind's attempts to master creation independently of the Creator (Gen 11:1–9). The builders attempted to define themselves by the achievement of their own efforts instead of by a co-operative relationship to God. What a mess resulted!

Ecclesiastes chapter 2 further highlights the frustration and seemingly pointless nature of work undertaken without reference to God:

Yet when I surveyed all that my hands had done
      and what I had toiled to achieve,
everything was meaningless, a chasing after the wind;
      nothing was gained under the sun...

So I hated life, because the work that is done under the sun was grievous to me. All of it is meaningless, a chasing after the wind. I hated all the things I had toiled for under the sun, because I must leave them to the one who comes after me ... For a man may do his work with wisdom, knowledge and skill, and then he must leave all he owns to someone who has not worked for it. This too is meaningless and a great misfortune. What does a man get for all the toil and anxious striving with which he labours under the sun? All his days his work is pain and grief; even at night his mind does not rest. This too is meaningless.

                                        (Ecclesiastes 2:11,17–19,21–23)

Redeeming the workplace

But God has not abandoned the workplace. Rather, he seeks to redeem the sphere of work just as he seeks to redeem every realm of human activity. And he invites believers to work with him in transforming their workplaces from a place of cursing (sometimes literally so!) back into places of blessing. How can we do this?

My first ever job was in a factory that provided prefabricated materials for the construction industry. For the first two weeks I did nothing but bang cork stoppers into the end of hollowed-out bolts. These bolts were known as 'whits', and as the ones I had to plug were half-inch size, the job was known as 'half-whit bashing'! From there I progressed to welding, which was less mind-numbing and more responsible. In the factory I wanted to be known as a Christian. The fact I was going on to study theology at Bible college made for some interesting conversations. ('Theology? Is that a bit like geology, then?') But mostly I contented myself with simply avoiding the kind of behaviour I regarded as unworthy of a Christian. My witness consisted mostly of the things I did not do: I did not swear (well, only under my breath when I bashed my thumb instead of one of the half-whits); I did not smoke; I did not skive off early or roll in late; and I tried very hard not to glance too often at the page-three-style calendar hanging on the wall.

The trouble is that this, together with leaving the odd tract in the works canteen, is about as far as many Christians ever get in trying to be a good witness at work. It is all rather negative. But we are also called to be a *positive* witness, to act as the kind of salt and light

Jesus describes in his sermon on the mount (Matt 5:13–16). Salt works unseen, but leaves its distinctive savour on whatever it makes contact with. Light, on the other hand, is highly visible and can be seen even at huge distances (think of the stars). So we should look for both low- and high-profile means of maintaining our Christian witness in the workplace.

'You are the salt of the earth'

When used as a preservative, as it was in many ancient cultures, salt needs to be rubbed in well. If a Christian is to be salt, he or she needs to get involved. The trouble with many Christians in the workplace is that they stand on the sidelines, fearful that if they get too close to the culture of their workplace, they may compromise their witness. Now I am not suggesting that we adopt some of the habits of our unconverted colleagues, but there are ways we can become more involved than we do. For example:

• Getting alongside the person everyone else dislikes;

• Helping the newcomer find his or her feet;

• Congratulating the person who gets the promotion you wanted;

• Spreading encouragement instead of gossip;

• Lending a confidential ear to the colleague whose marriage is falling apart.

In all of these ways we are working to re-humanise the workplace – something that is much needed in our time.

Building genuine relationships is the key, but sadly, within two years of becoming a believer, many Christians have no friends other than Christian ones and no social life beyond the church. This is a terrible indictment. Look at Jesus: he steadfastly refused to confine his time to religious or respectable people. We might be far more useful to the Lord going to the pub with our workmates now and again, and giving the Bible study or prayer meeting a miss once in a while.

A recent survey revealed that ten years ago the average person had six friends. Today, that figure is down to just three. Despite, or perhaps because of, the advent of modern communication technologies – the mobile phone, the Internet and email – people have fewer close relationships. We speak of 'virtual reality': it would be more accurate to describe life today as 'superficial reality'. Building real friendships is one of the best ways Christians can be effective witnesses in their workplaces. These friendships must be genuine and unconditional, and not merely for the sake of scalp-collecting. If they never lead to our non-Christian friends being won for Christ, then so be it. But remember – four out of five people who become Christians do so through the witness of a Christian friend.

Witnessing through lifestyle and relationships is a matter of common sense, involving faithfulness over a long period of time. There are more adventurous ways we can witness, too, which will involve a more courageous leap of faith.

Most Christians attend a church reasonably near their home, but the people they work with are likely to come from all over. Most will not live anywhere near the

church their Christian colleague is going to. But many
Christians think witnessing means inviting people to
church or church events! When Jesus gave his disciples
the great commission (Matt 28:16–20), he did not tell
them to invite their friends to come to church. Instead,
he told them to *go* 'and make disciples of all nations'. In
point of fact, there is not one example in the New
Testament where unbelievers were invited to church; it
was always the church that went to them.

And anyway, where is the church? On Sunday the
church of which I am pastor meets in a Victorian building off the High Street in Olney, a Buckinghamshire
market town. The church is there because the people are
there, worshipping God. But if you were to ask me the
same question on Monday morning, I would have to
give you a very different answer. The church, the Body
of Christ of which I am a part, will not be found in the
now empty building known as Olney Baptist Church. It
will be found scattered in homes, schools, colleges, hos-
pitals, offices, shops and factories over a radius of twenty miles or more. Some may even be overseas, either on
holiday or a foreign business trip.

Britain has a consulate or embassy in most countries
of the world, and an ambassador to represent British
interests abroad. A Christian at his or her place of work
is Christ's ambassador in that place. They are the
church in that office, factory, shop, school or wherever.
It is time we stopped thinking about how we can bring
our colleagues and workmates to church, and started
thinking about how we can bring the church to them.

This can be done in many ways. If there are several
Christians in the same workplace, would it be possible

to form a Christian Union? As well as being a mutual support to Christian believers, a CU can provide a platform for witness. Speakers (definitely not clergy) can be invited in to talk, from a Christian perspective, on a topic of general interest: coping with teenagers, maintaining a healthy lifestyle, money worries and the millennium are all topics that come to mind. Alternatively, a local celebrity – a sportsman or woman perhaps – with an up-to-date testimony could be invited to an informal lunchtime gathering.

What about a lunchtime enquirers' course? Would your boss mind if you borrowed a room to run an Alpha Course or something similar? Probably not. He or she might even be prepared to come along.

Perhaps you could pray for a sick colleague, or for a member of their family who is ill. Tell your colleague, without being pious about it, that you are praying. Better still – stick your neck right out and offer to pray with them for their healing.

Elijah and Obadiah

Some Christians will be more gifted towards a high-profile witness, while others will have a temperament more suited to a low-profile witness. The former may be happy to give an enthusiastic lead to launching a Christian Union or an Alpha Course; the latter will be more at ease witnessing quietly by befriending individuals and generally trying to make the working environment a more human and pleasant place to be. While one is acting as light, the other is acting as salt. Experience suggests that for every Christian who is able to make a

high-profile witness, there will be nine more who will be
better suited to low-profile witness. We should avoid
thinking that one is better than another. A common mistake is for Christians to try to do both and end up doing
neither very well.

The Old Testament story of Elijah is well-known.
We have already referred to his contest with the
prophets of Baal on Mount Carmel. But Elijah was not
the only person witnessing for his faith at that time. On
Mount Horeb, when Elijah was filled with self-doubt,
God told him that there were no fewer than 7,000 other
Israelites who had not bowed the knee to Baal (1 Kings
19:18). Among them was an unsung hero of faith:
Obadiah. His story is told in the first half of 1 Kings 18.

Obadiah is described as 'a devout believer in the
Lord' (v 3). His position was a difficult one because he
was also in charge of the palace of King Ahab who,
under the thumb of his wife Jezebel, was killing the
Lord's prophets and promoting the worship of Baal.
Obadiah had taken a hundred prophets and hidden
them in two caves, supplying them with food and water.
As far as Ahab was concerned Obadiah was a loyal worker, but as far as Obadiah was concerned his first loyalty
was to God. While Elijah expressed his loyalty to the
Lord through outright defiance, Obadiah expressed his
in hidden ways. It was not that Obadiah was a coward or
a compromiser: his gifts were organisational and practical, whereas Elijah's were public and upfront. Both
Elijah and Obadiah were exercising risk-taking faith,
but while one was demonstrating public adventurous
faith, the other was showing the value of a quieter, common-sense approach.

Witness in the workplace needs both Elijahs and Obadiahs. Neither has any reason to be suspicious or resentful of the other. Obadiah could not have done what Elijah did, but neither could Elijah have fulfilled Obadiah's calling. Each needed the other for the success of his particular ministry. If someone in our place of work witnesses in a very different style from the one with which we feel comfortable, we should not work against or ignore it. He or she deserves our support, prayers and encouragement.

Whether they adopt a high or a low profile, every Christian is called to give personal witness to Jesus Christ. Sometimes we can create an opportunity to share our faith; at other times we can only pray and wait for opportunities to come. Whenever and however they come, they are best taken simply and naturally. Of course, what we say needs to be backed up by the highest standards of moral and ethical integrity, as well as our warmth, concern and care.

One final word of advice here. When there is an opportunity to share your faith at work, don't talk about church. Talk about Jesus instead. If your church did something out of the ordinary over the weekend – the kind of thing people do not normally associate with their preconceived idea of church – then perhaps it is worth mentioning. But people do not want to hear your account of the minister's sermon on The Problems Encountered by Paul on his Third Missionary Journey. It will be a real turn-off and only serve to reinforce the stereotypical image most unbelievers have of what goes on inside most church buildings.

Talk about Jesus instead of church. Let it be known

that you have a living friendship with him. Don't be religious: be human. Don't engage in hit-and-run smile-Jesus-loves-you evangelism: cultivate relationships. Don't judge: listen. Then you will earn the right to speak.

Failing everything else, you could try putting a tract in every pair of shoes that you sell, every order that leaves your factory or every letter that leaves your office. But I would not recommend it.

❧ Notes

1. Mark Greene, *Thank God it's Monday*, Scripture Union, 1997, p 19.

❧ Further reading

Mark Greene, *Thank God it's Monday*, Scripture Union, 1997.

Geoff Shattock, *Wake up to Work*, Scripture Union, 1999.

Graham Dow, *A Christian Understanding of Daily Work*, Grove Books, 1994.

❧ Questions to think about

1. How has this chapter changed your attitude towards your job (whether this is paid employment, voluntary work, or looking after home and family)?

2. Do you have a tendency to compartmentalise your life into 'spiritual' and 'secular'? If so, how could this be corrected?

3. How could your church better support its members in their daily occupations?

4. How might more faith or more common sense help you to make or maintain a Christian witness in your particular place of work?

Chapter Eight

MONEY MATTERS

It would be hard, almost impossible, to imagine life without money. It makes the world go round, or so the song says. But money worries can also bring our little world grinding to a halt. It is not just a question of how much or how little we have, but how tightly we cling to the feet of this false god.

We like to think of our money as – well, just that – *ours*. Our bank statements inform us how much we have in our account. Our pay-slips declare how much we are earning. Bills and credit card statements remind us what it is we have bought with our precious money (and it's usually a painful experience!). But is our money really ours?

We like to imagine that money gives us independence – we can go where we want, buy what we want, do what we want. But the Bible insists that the money in our wallet, purse or bank account is a reminder of the exact opposite – not our independence but our *dependence* on God.

In an ultimate sense, even if we earn our own living, we are all dependent on God. It is God who gives us the physical strength and mental skills we need to earn that living. To imagine otherwise is arrogant folly.

> You may say to yourself, 'My power and the strength of my hands have produced this wealth for me.' But remember the Lord your God, for it is he who gives you the ability to produce wealth...'
>
> *(Deuteronomy 8:17–18)*

Jesus once told a story about a get-rich-quick farmer:

> 'The ground of a certain rich man produced a good crop. He thought to himself, "What shall I do? I have no place to store my crops."
>
> 'Then he said: "This is what I'll do. I will tear down my barns and build bigger ones, and there I will store all my grain and my goods. And I'll say to myself, 'You have plenty of good things laid up for many years. Take life easy; eat, drink and be merry.' "
>
> 'But God said to him, 'You fool! This very night your life will be demanded from you. Then who will get what you have prepared for yourself?'
>
> *(Luke 12:13–21)*

The rich man's money and possessions counted for nothing in the end. He had forgotten that life can only be lived in dependence on God. All that we have comes through his provision in creation: 'The earth is the Lord's and everything in it' (Psalm 24:1). But we can live in dependence on God either indirectly or directly. Direct dependence on God is sometimes called 'living by faith', and we will look at this first.

Living by faith

In a sense, all of life is meant to be lived 'by faith' (2 Cor 5:7); but when Christian workers – missionaries mostly – talk about 'living by faith', they mean living without a guaranteed means of support, usually in order to undertake some form of Christian service. I have had the opportunity to 'live by faith' in this way on two occasions. On the first, I accepted the challenge and spent almost a year praying in my finances. On the second, I said no and walked away. Why did I accept the one and not the other?

The first opportunity came when I was nineteen and had just started at Romsey House, then a small theological college in Cambridge. At the end of my first term I was given the chance of extending my time there by a year, which would enable me to do the extra subjects I wanted to study, including Old Testament Hebrew (though whatever made me want to do that particular subject I cannot now imagine!). I contacted the local education authority that had awarded my grant. 'By all means extend your studies,' they told me, 'but we can't extend the money!' If I was to do the extra year, I would have to accept a suspension of my grant with immediate effect.

I spoke to the pastor and others in my home church. They encouraged me to take advantage of the extra study. Though they could not guarantee any financial help, they indicated that some might be possible. So I accepted the challenge of living by faith for a year and began to pray for the funds I needed (a total of about £800, not altogether an inconsiderable sum in 1975!).

Bit by bit the money came in: some from individuals, some from the church, some from totally unexpected quarters. Gifts ranged from £5 to over £100. In the
summer break I was able to take a temporary factory job
as a welder which, together with further gifts in the
autumn, took me through to the end of the year and the
resumption of my grant. As a relatively new Christian,
it was a wonderful lesson to learn that my loving heavenly Father could meet all my earthly needs.

The second opportunity to 'live by faith' came six
years later. I was nearing the end of my training for the
ordained ministry at the South Wales Baptist College in
Cardiff, and I was invited to consider a position as pastor of a small chapel in the Welsh valleys. The chapel
harked back to the glory days of the 1905 Welsh Revival
but had been in decline ever since. This decline was now
nearly terminal. Most of the existing members were
elderly, with few wage-earners among them. The chapel
was set in an area of industrial and social decay: the clo-
sure of one coal pit after another had left many unem-
ployed, and there was a constant stream of people
moving away in search of work elsewhere.

Having preached there 'with a view' to accepting the
appointment, I was given a conducted tour of the
church premises by the church secretary. Until now,
nothing had been said about money. I decided it was
time to ask. Looking round the dilapidated state of the
buildings, I was beginning to wonder whether they had
any and could afford to pay a minister. In hushed tones,
the secretary explained their position. They had saved
enough to pay a pastor for six months, but after that the
money would run out. 'But,' he said, 'any minister

worth his salt would, in those six months, be able to increase the congregation sufficiently to ensure more respectable offerings and a future for the church.' I would be living by faith, he said. 'Yes,' I thought. 'My faith, not yours.'

A few days later I wrote to the secretary explaining that I did not feel 'led' to explore the possibility any further. Was this a lack of faith on my part? Had my faith grown weaker instead of stronger in the six years since Cambridge? Was I going soft as a Christian, or was it something else?

God can, of course, do the seemingly impossible. Revival could have broken out in those six months in the Welsh chapel (though I never heard that it did), and God could have provided for my needs there. Why then had I decided to walk away from the challenge?

Well, faith, even adventurous faith, should not be based on unreality. Believing that God can do the humanly impossible is different from believing that he makes fairytales come true. Dreams and visions, yes – fairytales, no. Faith is not about believing six impossible things before breakfast, as the Queen of Hearts suggested to Alice in Lewis Carroll's *Through the Looking-Glass*. Genuine faith does not seek to escape from reality. Instead, it faces up to a situation realistically and seeks a way through. While faith may come to a different conclusion from common sense, it should never ignore common sense.

When I declined the invitation to pastor the church, it was more a gut reaction than anything else, but it was a gut reaction supported by certain principles. First, it was evident that the church expected *me* to be the one with the faith. Now there have been missionaries who have 'gone solo', living on their faith alone as they have pioneered a blazing trail for the gospel in some remote jungle or mountain pass. But when there are other Christians around, God expects faith to be something that is shared among them. If that church was serious about growth, about evangelism, about calling a pastor – then where was the evidence of their faith? As far as I could see, there was very little. I would have been making all the sacrifices and taking all the risks, while they stood on the sidelines, looking on from a position of relative safety.

Faith can never be an abdication of responsibility. Faith relies on God for what we *can't* do, not for what we *won't* do. Faith is not an alternative to sacrificial effort and sheer hard work. Genuine faith will always issue in obedience and sacrifice that is shared by *all* those whom God calls to a particular venture.

Second, the prospects for growth had to be assessed with some realism. A quick calculation suggested that it would be necessary, in those first six months, to bring to the Lord at least twenty wage-earning people and, within that same time frame, to persuade each of them to start tithing (giving ten per cent of their income) to the church. Half would be needed to pay for a minister's stipend, and the other half to cover the running expenses of the church. But this church was in an area of high unemployment, where it was notoriously difficult to get people of working age, particularly men, to worship. Even if twenty wage-earning men could be converted within six months, pastoral experience suggests that it takes considerably longer than that before most new

Christians acquire the habit of regular giving, let alone tithing. Conversion of the soul is one thing; conversion of the pocket is quite another!

Third, however great God may be, I know my limitations. Nearly twenty years in the pastoral ministry since my decision not to go to that Welsh valley have confirmed that my gifts lie in the areas of teaching and pastoral care, and not primarily in evangelism. What this Welsh chapel needed was Billy Graham. The Archangel Gabriel would have been even better! What they did not need was me – a college boy still wet behind the ears.

Fourth, I was about to get married. Taking a risk of faith that affects only oneself is one thing; making a decision that will affect someone else is a much greater responsibility. Perhaps I could have lived in one room, eaten cold baked beans and prepared my sermons by candlelight. But it was no place to start married life or consider raising a family.

Occasionally, perhaps once or twice in a lifetime, God will call a Christian to 'live by faith' in direct dependence on him. This might take the form of living without a guaranteed income or it might be a little less radical – leaving one job without the certainty of another, for example, or moving from better to less well-paid employment, or giving away a substantial one-off sum from your savings which had been earmarked for something else. But whether or not God ever calls us to 'live by faith', he always calls us to live faithfully and obediently in the area of financial management, exercising wise and common-sense stewardship of what we keep and a generosity of spirit in what we release for his service.

But before we unpack what it means to live in *indirect* dependence on God, it will be helpful to consider two biblical examples of God's provision, one of direct dependence on him, the other of indirect dependence.

God the provider

God is our provider, but he can provide for us in any number of ways. Sometimes it will be through direct intervention, but more often it will be through indirect means.

The Bible shows God's special concern for the vulnerable, which includes orphans, widows and those it calls 'resident aliens' (people forced to live in a country other than their homeland). During a time of drought and famine in the region, Elijah the prophet was directed by God to go to Zarephath in Sidon, to the house of a widow (1 Kings 17:7–24). The widow was living in extreme poverty, struggling to get by on very little. However, she was generous to share what she had with Elijah. He, in return, was able to work a miracle for her, promising her that her jar of flour and jug of oil would not run out until the day the famine ended. For perhaps three years the widow lived in direct dependence on God. This was a daily reminder for her of God's provision, similar to that of the quail and manna which he had given to the Israelites as they wandered in the desert during the time of Moses (Num 11).

As well as her daily food, God provided for the widow in a moment of crisis. One day her only son collapsed and died. Without a man around the place, the woman would have had great difficulty in fending for herself. However, in response to her desperate plea for help, Elijah prayed and the boy was miraculously restored to life.

When Jesus commented on this story in his teaching, he made an important point: 'that there were many widows in Israel in Elijah's time, when the sky was shut for three and a half years and there was a severe famine throughout the land. Yet Elijah was not sent to any of them, but to a widow in Zarephath in the region of Sidon' (Luke 4:25-26). The widow was the only person in the region to be helped in this way; moreover, she was a Gentile and not a Jew. The miraculous intervention of God to provide directly for our needs is the exception and not the norm.

The more normal pattern is for God to provide indirectly, as he did for Ruth, whose story we looked at in chapter two. God provided her and her mother-in-law, Naomi, with food for them both and a husband for Ruth. But the provision was not supernatural in any way. Instead it came about through a combination of three factors: the hard work and courageous initiative of the two widows themselves; the framework of God-given laws that, at the time, helped to create a just and fair society; and the generosity of God's people, most notably, in this instance, of Boaz who married Ruth. But there are no miracles. The only hint of direct divine intervention in the story comes at the beginning of the story, when we are told that God had brought Bethlehem's famine to an end (Ruth 1:6).

While the story of the widow of Zarephath highlights the 'otherness' or transcendence of God, the story of Ruth stresses his 'nearness' or immanence.

Occasionally we may be called or may need to live in
direct dependence on God. The more usual pattern,
however, is that we should live in indirect dependence
on him through earning a living by the effort of our own
hands.

In the remainder of this chapter we will look at our
attitude to money – the money we keep and the money
we give away.

The money we give away

There is not the space to unpack all the Bible has to say
about giving, but it is worthwhile reminding ourselves
of some basic principles. Since we have mentioned giving and tithing, let's start there.

Tithing, giving a tenth of our income, is a principle
found in the Old Testament. It is first mentioned in connection with Abraham, who made an offering of a tenth
of the goods he had recovered in battle while rescuing his
nephew Lot (Gen 14:18–20). Abraham's gift was not
given out of any sense of legal duty (the law of Moses, in
which tithing is commanded, was still several hundred
years in the future, see Lev 27:30–33), but out of joy and
thankfulness. This point is worth remembering by those
who say tithing is something legalistic: Abraham gave a
tithe because he wanted to, not because he had to.

Even when we do turn to the law of Moses, we find
that tithing was a only a baseline for giving. Freewill and
other offerings were made on top. Generosity began at
eleven per cent!

It is true that Jesus never commanded tithing, but he
never said the practice should be discontinued either!

He did indeed criticise those who were over-scrupulous about it to the extent of tithing their herbs and spices, but who neglected the 'weightier matters' of love and justice (Matt 23:23–24). However, this does not negate the principle of tithing for Christians. The principle should be applied as a guideline and a starting point to all our giving, but exercised with a joyful freedom of spirit. How can we, who are the beneficiaries of God's gift of Jesus to the world, give back to God less than the Old Testament Israelites who knew nothing of Jesus?

The apostle Paul encouraged the Christians at Corinth and Galatia to put aside a gift at the beginning of each week and to save this up until he could collect it and take it to the needy church in Jerusalem (1 Cor 16:1–4). He urges them to give generously and not grudgingly: 'each person should give what he has decided in his heart to give, not reluctantly or under compulsion, for God loves a cheerful giver' (2 Cor 9:5). Generous and cheerful giving is part of what it means to exercise faith. Sometimes that faith will be adventurous and spontaneous, perhaps through the sacrificial giving of a large, one-off sum of money. At other times, it will be a matter of daily obedience, with regular planned giving, thought through prayerfully and on the basis of biblical principles such as tithing. Either way, our generosity and joy will be an expression of our trust in God who has so generously given us all that we have.

The money we keep

So, we are to be generous and cheerful in our giving, but what about the 90 per cent of our income that remains in our pockets? Knowing what to do with this is often more problematic than knowing how much to give away.

Here, too, the Bible is not short on guidelines. First, we must realise that what we keep is as much God's as what we give away. The offertory prayer in the Church of England's *Alternative Service Book 1980* says, 'Yours, Lord, is the greatness, the power, the glory, the splendour, and the majesty; for everything in heaven and earth is yours. All things come from you, and of your own do we give you.' Recognition of this fact should engender within us an attitude of constant thankfulness. Such a spirit of thankfulness encourages us to remember our dependency on God and, at the same time, to worry less and to be more trusting of our heavenly Father.

As well as adopting an attitude of thankfulness, the Bible also encourages an attitude of healthy suspicion towards money and possessions. Money can make life more comfortable in a thousand ways, but it can never fully satisfy our deepest needs. Even if we have a fortune, it cannot provide all the security we want. It cannot buy peace of mind. It cannot promise a happy family life or success in relationships. It cannot guarantee or buy good health. And, of course, however much we have, we cannot take it with us.

> Naked I came from my mother's womb, and naked I will depart.
>
> *(Job 1:21)*

> For we brought nothing into the world, and we can take nothing out of it.
>
> *(1 Timothy 6:7)*

Someone once asked the multi-millionaire J D Rockefeller how much money it would take to satisfy him. 'Just a little bit more,' he replied. He would have agreed with the Old Testament philosopher who said, 'Whoever loves money never has enough; whoever loves wealth is never satisfied with his income' (Eccl 5:10). We live in a world full of advertising slogans shouting out the lie that more possessions means more happiness. This constant desire for what we do not have is what the Bible calls *covetousness*. 'But godliness with contentment is great gain' (1 Tim 6:6).

How do we fight back against our attachment to money, to things and to possessions? How do we counteract the spirit of greed and covetousness which our society so readily encourages and so often endorses? Here are ideas you might consider:

• Buy things for their usefulness, not for their status or to keep up with fashion.

• Avoid impulse buying. Decide what you need before you go shopping and stick to your list. An occasional treat or surprise is fine, but not too often. If you see something you fancy which you had not thought of buying before you left home, leave it for another day. This will help you decide if you really need it.

• Avoid 'buy now, pay later' schemes. Save up instead.

• Consider second-hand as an alternative to buying new. Mend rather than replace. Recycle where possible. When it comes to buying a car, it is more economical to buy 'nearly new' (one to two years old) than brand new; then keep the same car for four to five years before trading it in.

- Resist advertising propaganda. Despite suggestions to the contrary, washing your hair with Brand X shampoo or drinking Brand Y coffee is *not* likely to make you irresistible to members of the opposite sex!

- Admit to your weaknesses and resist buying whatever it is you find most addictive. This includes chocolate!

- Borrow or share instead of purchasing. Think about borrowing that book or CD from the library as an alternative to feeling you must have your own. Take turns driving to work with a colleague, or share the school-run with a neighbour.

The things mentioned here are guidelines, not rigid rules. God wants us to live in the freedom of his Spirit, not in slavery to human-made regulations. But he does want us to exercise common sense and Bible-guided faithfulness in our budgeting, spending and saving, as we learn to trust God and be generous towards others, and just perhaps take a bigger than usual risk with our future and our financial security.

✒ Further reading

Richard Foster, *Celebration of Discipline*, Hodder and Stoughton, 1980.

Foster, *Freedom of Simplicity*, Triangle/SPCK, 1981.

Foster, *Money, Sex and Power*, Hodder and Stoughton, 1985.

Money for God's Sake, Evangelical Alliance/Credit Action, 1993.

Keith Tondeur, *What Jesus Said About Money and Possessions*, Monarch, 1998.

A wide range of books and materials offering practical help with budget-making and debt-solving is available from Credit Action, 6 Regent Terrace, Cambridge CB2 1AA.

ℰ Questions to think about

1. Do you think your attitude to money relies more on faith or on common sense? Why?

2. Under what circumstances might you be prepared to trust God for your income?

3. Jesus said, 'Do not store up for yourselves treasures on earth, where moth and rust destroy, and where thieves break in and steal. But store up for yourselves treasures in heaven, where moth and rust do not destroy, and where thieves do not break in and steal. For where your treasure is, there your heart will be also' (Matt 6:19–21).

    What do you think he was getting at? How attached are you to your money and possessions? How does this affect your spiritual growth? (Read the whole of Matthew 6:19–34.)

Chapter Nine

FAITH AND FAILURE

A few weeks before I sat down to write this chapter, the churches in Olney, the market town where I minister, held a united evangelistic event. We invited a gifted Christian actress, Julie-Ann Hilton, to perform a play in which she portrays twelve women from the Bible. Her performance was excellent and the play had a hard-hitting message. The only trouble was that the audience numbered no more than two dozen, and the vast majority of them were church members. Financially, we lost nearly £250 on the venture. We had done everything right: the play had been well-publicised and church members had been urged to bring their non-Christian friends. The few who did come looked a pitiful sight in a church that can accommodate several hundred, but at least everyone had a front row seat!

Some would say that number-counting is unspiritual, as indeed it can be. They might also point out that we can never know what seed might have been sown, and even if only one unbeliever was touched or one believer moved to deeper commitment, then it was all worthwhile. Others would say that we must have got our guidance wrong. Maybe it was a good idea, but not God's idea. Although the play had been a sell-out in dozens of other venues and wonderfully used to speak to believers and unbelievers alike, perhaps God had in mind a different method of evangelising Olney.

Hindsight is all very well, as is finding a 'spiritual' explanation for the small audience. But the fact of the matter is, our evangelistic venture was a failure. In plain English, *it did not work*. Short and simple.

This is a relatively trivial example. We learnt whatever lessons needed to be learnt and moved on. But Christians encounter failure all the time. Believers can and do fail. They fail exams. They fail in job applications. They fail in business ventures. They fail in personal relationships. They sometimes fail in ministry.

I have had three pastorates. My first, in Sheffield, could by most standards be judged a success. My third, here in Olney, is going well so far. (At least I think so!) But whatever my second pastorate was, it was *not* successful. I inherited a situation in which the church – near the New Forest in Hampshire – was divided and discouraged. For four years I poured everything into it, but every time one division was healed, another broke out elsewhere. Every time we were nearing agreement about a way forward in mission and evangelism, there would be yet another attack on my ministry from one quarter or another.

Now maybe I did manage to draw out some of the poison that was infecting the church. Maybe I did make life easier for the minister who followed. I do not know. What I do know is that every step forward felt as though it was matched by two steps back. At the end of four years, I was not at all sure I even wanted to be in the Baptist ministry.

Don't get me wrong. Along the way there were successes. There were those who came to faith, there were baptisms, and there were those who found personal renewal of their faith despite the hurts the church had inflicted upon them. However, overall, the verdict of my time in the New Forest must be that it was a failure, not a success. Although I made mistakes, I did my best and was faithful in ministry, but it was not enough to overcome the self-imposed problems the church was facing.

Failure and sin

Let's get one thing straight: all sin is failure, but not all failure is sin. Failure can be the result of personal sin, but it can also be the result of many other factors. Let's take some examples.

A church decides to open a Christian bookshop. It needs an annual turnover of £25,000 to remain financially viable. But, after five years, the turnover is still only £10,000 and the shop has to close. Perhaps there was an initial misjudgement of the projected sales, or perhaps during the five years an unexpected recession hit the retail book trade. Was it wrong to have opened the shop? Was there a mistake in hearing God's guidance? Not necessarily.

A student does his best but still fails his exams. Perhaps he was unwisely advised about entering the exam. But in failing, he has discovered his level of academic achievement and may still have benefited from the course in some way. Was he wrong to have entered for the exam in the first place? Again, not necessarily.

We may fail through unforeseen circumstances – ill health, the resignation of a key worker – a hundred and one possibilities may force a change of plan or even the abandonment of a particular project. We may also fail because of the unforeseen response of others. Jim Elliot and four others went as missionaries to an unevangelised tribe in South America. At their first contact, all five men were killed by the tribesmen. Were they wrong to go? Not at all, as the later success of their widows to win the tribe to Christ bears eloquent testimony.

We had better get used to it. Failure comes with being part of a fallen world. It is, as they say, part of the territory, and the Christian is not immune from it. Failure is by no means always a sign of sin, unfaithfulness or disobedience on the part of the believer. Christians, especially evangelicals, fear failure. They will often do nothing rather than risk failure. What they do not realise is that doing nothing is itself failure – failure to engage in the mission to which God calls us. As the nineteenth-century English poet, Arthur H Clough, wrote, ''Tis better to have fought and lost, Than never to have fought at all.'

In 1998 the church of which I am minister embarked on its first Alpha Course (the popular Christian enquirers' course written by Nicky Gumbel of Holy Trinity, Brompton, in London). For a long time, we discussed the pros and cons of holding such a course. One church member asked, 'How do we know it will succeed?' I replied that we did not and could not know if it would succeed. Neither I nor anyone else could guarantee success. 'If we knew for certain that it would be a success,' I explained, 'we would not need faith.' Faith always risks failure. That said, in my experience, plans born out of prayer and borne by prayer are more likely to succeed than those in which prayer is either absent or an afterthought.

'Not by might nor by power, but by my Spirit,' says the LORD Almighty.

(Zechariah 4:6)

Unless the LORD builds the house,
 its builders labour in vain.

(Psalm 127:1)

Peter revisited

This brings us back to our friend Peter. In chapter one, we saw that when he got out of the boat, his doubt was showing as much as his faith. He was uncertain as to whether it actually was Jesus he could see through the wind and waves. Then, when he took his eyes off Jesus, his doubts got the better of his faith and he started to sink. Mercifully, Jesus rescued him and they walked back to the boat together.

It is said that a man's past life flashes before him when he is drowning. I wonder what Peter was thinking as the water rose around him. 'I should have stayed in that boat. Better still, I should have stayed at home!' Or perhaps he began to wonder what his fellow disciples might be saying at his funeral. 'That Peter, he always was too reckless for his own good.' It would have made a nice epitaph:

Here lies the body of impetuous Pete
who jumped overboard in his sandalled feet.

Peter did not drown, but at least he had taken a risk where the other disciples had refused. He had got out of the boat while they stayed firmly inside. If his wave-walking episode was a failure, then I for one would not mind a few failures like that! But Peter learnt some important lessons from his near-failure, and they are lessons we – if you will forgive the pun – must take on board too.

First, success and failure are often mixed. Projects we embark on will very rarely, if ever, be a one-hundred-percent success or a one-hundred-percent failure. If we stay in the boat, we will know neither success nor failure. If we step out, we will know a measure of both.

Second, Peter learnt humility. Success can bring with it more problems than failure. Success brings pride, and pride can engender a false sense of self-reliance. We may feel we have achieved something, and start thinking that we can achieve success without God. And this leads to ingratitude towards God.

When Amaziah, King of Judah, succeeded in defeating the people of Edom without the help he had asked for from Jehoash, King of Israel, he became proud of his success (2 Chron 25). He forgot that it had come from God; indeed, in his arrogance he began worshipping other gods. God sent a prophet to warn Amaziah (v 16). Jehoash also spoke to him: 'You say to yourself that you have defeated Edom, and now you are arrogant and proud. But stay at home! Why ask for trouble and cause your own downfall and that of Judah also?' (v 19). Later Amaziah met Jehoash (now an enemy, not an ally) in battle, and Amaziah was roundly defeated. His reign ended in disaster when he was assassinated by conspirators from his own side.

When they marched into Canaan, following God's instructions and with his direct intervention, the Israelites triumphed against all the odds and took the city of Jericho (Josh 2–6). Flushed with success, they thought they could do the same again to the next city, Ai. But complacency had set in and the people suggested to Joshua that only a small number of men need be involved in the attack. However, instead of success, their attack was an unmitigated disaster and they were soundly routed by the soldiers of Ai (Josh 7:3–5). Deep repentance was necessary before they could make a second attack.

> Pride goes before destruction, a haughty spirit before a fall.
>
> *(Proverbs 16:18).*

The lesson of humility that Peter learnt on Lake Galilee was important for his entire future. Pride could easily have set in on so many occasions – when 3,000 people were converted on the day of Pentecost (Acts 2); when the crippled beggar leapt to his feet (Acts 3); when Dorcas was raised to life (Acts 9); when the Holy Spirit was bestowed on the people of Samaria (Acts 8). But years later Peter was to write: 'Humble yourselves, therefore, under God's mighty hand, that he may lift you up in due time. Cast all your anxiety on him because he cares for you' (1 Pet 5:6–7). As he wrote this, was he remembering the day when Jesus caught his arm and saved him from a watery fate? Or was he thinking of the night Jesus was arrested, when he failed in a much more serious way?

Only hours earlier, at the last supper, Peter had sworn his loyalty: 'Even if all fall away on account of you, I never will.' He must have been hurt by Jesus' reply:

> I tell you the truth,' Jesus answered, 'this very night, before the cock crows, you will disown me three times.'
> But Peter declared, 'Even if I have to die with you, I will never disown you.' And all the other disciples said the same.
>
> *(Matthew 26:33–35)*

But Jesus' fearful prediction came true – not because Peter had no choice in the matter, but because Jesus knew him so well. He knew that, too often, Peter spoke before putting his brain in gear. Within hours he had, as predicted, disowned his Lord three times. As the third occasion passed and the cock crowed, Jesus' words came flooding back. Peter went away and 'wept bitterly' (v 75).

But Peter had one thing going for him, and this brings us to the third lesson he learnt – failure was not the end. He could fail and still be loved by the Lord. God was faithful even if he was not. The final chapter of John's Gospel tells the touching story of Peter's comeback.

Not knowing how to fulfil their new calling of fishing for people, Peter and the other Galilean disciples had gone back to fishing for fish. But this was proving a frustrating failure. All night not even a sardine swam into their nets. Then at dawn they saw a stranger on the shore. The stranger called out to them and they recognised his voice: 'It is the Lord!' It all must have seemed eerily familiar!

Jesus told them to throw the net out of the opposite side of the boat. They obeyed and hauled in their largest ever catch. Once again Peter jumped into the water (but this time it was shallow).

After they had hauled the fish ashore, Jesus invited them to join him for breakfast:

> When they had finished eating, Jesus said to Simon Peter, 'Simon son of John, do you truly love me more than these?'
>
> 'Yes, Lord,' he said, 'you know that I love you.'
>
> Jesus said, 'Feed my lambs.'
>
> Again Jesus said, 'Simon son of John, do you truly love me?'
>
> He answered, 'Yes, Lord, you know that I love you.'
>
> Jesus said, 'Take care of my sheep.'
>
> The third time he said to him, 'Simon son of John, do you love me?'
>
> Peter was hurt because Jesus asked him the third time, 'Do you love me?' He said, 'Lord, you know all things; you know that I love you.'
>
> *(John 21:15–17)*

Peter had denied the Lord three times. Jesus invites him three times to reaffirm his faith. Peter is restored and given another commission; in fact, he is given new responsibility – to pastor God's flock, which would soon be given over to his care.

There is no venture of genuine faith that does not run the risk of failure. While the godly person may expect to be more successful than others (Psalm 1:3) and is encouraged to pray for success (Gen 24:12; Neh 1:11), success does not belong to the believer as of right. We are never immune from failure. Some believe and even preach the notion that we can secure a life without risk so long as we remain in the will of God. In an ultimate, eternal sense, we may indeed be beyond risk, but this is not so in this life. In the superheated furnace, Daniel's three friends felt confident of God's protection. Nevertheless, they told Nebuchadnezzar, 'If we are thrown into the blazing furnace, the God we serve is able to save us from it, and he will rescue us from your hand, O king. But even if he does not, we want you to know, O king, that we will not serve your gods or worship the image of gold you have set up' (Dan 3:17–18).

If there is no risk, there is no faith. Worse, when Christians suggest that faith and certainty about God's will guarantee risk-free living, they are implying that those who fail or meet with risk have sinned in some way and have missed God's 'perfect will'. The apostle Paul writes:

> Do not conform any longer to the pattern of this world, but be transformed by the renewing of your mind. Then you will be able to test and approve what God's will is – his good, pleasing and perfect will.
>
> *(Romans 12:2)*

Commenting on this passage, Dallas Willard says:[1]

> It is absolutely essential to the nature of human development towards maturity that we venture and be placed at risk. *Only risk produces character.* ... In truth, we need not seek risk, but we will never be without it – at least in this world. Nor should we try to be.

Faith and common sense

Common sense dictates that we should do all we reasonably can to minimise the risk of failure – to do otherwise is to put God to the test. The person who drives his car knowing the brakes are faulty, or who goes sailing without a lifejacket, is acting presumptuously, taking God's promised protective care for granted.

Common sense says that we should not be lazy but instead prepare as best we can. Common sense says we should use our experience and wisest judgement to weigh the pros and cons of every situation:

> 'Suppose one of you wants to build a tower. Will he not first sit down and estimate the cost to see if he has enough money to complete it? For if he lays the foundation and is not able to finish it, everyone who sees it will ridicule him, saying, "This fellow began to build and was not able to finish."
>
> 'Or suppose a king is about to go to war against another king. Will he not first sit down and consider whether he is able with ten thousand men to oppose the one coming against him with twenty thousand?'
>
> *(Luke 14: 28–31)*

Faith makes its calculations as well, but it also brings the power and guidance of God into the equation. Sometimes faith and common sense will come to the same conclusion as to whether or not it is prudent to embark upon a certain course of action. At other times, faith will come to a very different conclusion. Common sense said that it was not sensible for Gideon to take three hundred men into battle against the overwhelming might of the Midian army (Judges 7), for David to

tackle Goliath (1 Sam 17), or for Peter to get out of the
boat. But in each case, faith, albeit weak and the size of
a mustard seed, could see what God could do for the
honour of his name.

The story of Esther brings faith and common sense
together in a wonderful way. Esther, a Jewess, had been
crowned queen by the Persian king Ahasuerus (also
known as Xerxes). Then her cousin Mordecai uncov-
ered a genocidal plot to kill all the Jews living under
Persian rule. Esther was ideally placed to intercede on
their behalf, but approaching the king was risky. Catch
him on an off-day and it was likely to be 'off with your
head'.

Esther made sensible preparations for the meeting.
She fasted and prayed, and called on all the Jews living
locally to do the same (Esth 4:15–16). She put on her most
attractive royal robes and prepared two splendid banquets
(undoubtedly following the principle that the best way to
a king's heart is, as with most men, through his stomach).
Only then did she make her request that her people be
spared (7:3–4). Esther was as clever as she was beautiful
and she used every ounce of her savvy and her feminine
charms to her advantage. But she was still taking a huge
risk. Her predecessor, Queen Vashti, had been deposed by
the king in a pique of temper, and Esther knew that the
same or worse could easily happen to her. But, after all her
careful preparations, she could only hope: 'When this is
done, I will go to the king, even though it is against the law.
And if I perish, I perish' (4:16).

As it happened, Esther's life was spared and the Jews
were saved. But stories of faith do not always have such
a happy ending, at least when they are judged from a

human point of view. The first Christian martyr, Stephen, made a brave stand before the Sanhedrin (the Jewish High Council) in defence of his faith, but was nevertheless stoned to death (Acts 7). And, while Peter was miraculously delivered from prison by an angel, his colleague James was not so fortunate: Herod had him executed (Acts 12). James became the first of the apostolic band to die at the hands of persecutors.

The key phrase in the preceding paragraph is, of course, '*from a human point of view*'. From such a viewpoint, Stephen and James did fail; but from God's viewpoint their lives and their deaths were a resounding victory and a wonderful witness. What the world counts as failure, God often counts as success.

The ultimate measure of success or failure is the cross and resurrection of Jesus Christ. From a worldly viewpoint, Jesus' mission was a failure, a flame that flickered for a mere three years before being snuffed out in the most dishonourable form of death imaginable, on a wooden stake planted in the ground before the sneers and jeers of a watching crowd. But in Philippians 2, Paul tells us that our attitude should be the same as his:

> Who, being in very nature God,
>> did not consider equality with God something
>>> to be grasped,
> but made himself nothing,
>> taking the very nature of a servant,
>> being made in human likeness.
> And being found in appearance as a man,
>> he humbled himself
>> and became obedient to death – even death on
>>> a cross!
> Therefore God exalted him to the highest place

and gave him the name that is above every name,
that at the name of Jesus every knee should bow,
in heaven and on earth and under the earth,
and every tongue confess that Jesus Christ is Lord,
to the glory of God the Father.

If that is failure, give me failure every time!

❧ Notes

1. Dallas Willard, *Hearing God,* Fount (an imprint of HarperCollins Publishers), 1999, p 204 (his italics).

❧ Further reading

Dennis Lennon, *Weak Enough for God to Use*,
    Scripture Union, 1999.
Russ Parker, *Free to Fail*, SPCK/Triangle, 1999.

❧ Questions to think about

1. Have you ever had an experience of failure? What do you think was the cause? How did you feel about it, and how did it affect your faith?

2. To what extent should we expect Christians to live in perpetual victory?

3. How does the fact of the cross and resurrection of Jesus relate to failure and common sense?

Chapter Ten

FAITH AND GOD'S GUIDANCE

Jo, a church member, has given me permission to tell her story of God's guidance.

Jo had reached a plateau in her life. She had achieved a senior position in her nursing career. She had a mortgage, lots of friends and was settled in a church. But the future looked grim. What she really wanted was a husband. So she put this challenge to God: if her desire for a husband was not to be, then she wanted God to help her feel content with that and to direct her towards something worthwhile in her life for him. Jo 'let go' of her pursuit of a partner.

Soon afterwards, what she calls 'a series of coincidences' led her to volunteer for a two-week nursing assignment with a Christian charity in Romania. Church members asked why she was going. Jo's reply was that she felt it would lead to 'something significant', possibly a long-term placement in Romania. However, while the brief time in Romania was, in her words, 'challenging and uplifting' and taught her lessons of daily reliance upon God, she came home without any sense of being led towards a longer commitment. Had she got

her guidance wrong? She was confused as to why, apart
from the nursing help she had given, she had been guided to go, especially as she was so convinced that this trip
had long-term importance.

The trip did indeed have significance, but not in the
way Jo planned. While in Romania, Jeff, a freelance pho-
tographer from Devon, spent two days photographing
the project Jo was involved in. He too was making a brief
trip to Romania with the thought of offering his skills on
a more permanent basis. By now you will have guessed
how the story ends. On their return to England, romance
blossomed. Jo and Jeff are now married and have two
children. We will come back to their story a little later –
I want to make some comments on it. But first it is time
to do away with some misconceptions about guidance.

Push-button guidance?

In recent years, dozens of books have been published on
guidance. A large number of them focus on technique and
method. They read rather like D-I-Y manuals and have
titles like 'Knowing God's Will in Ten Easy Steps' or
'Guidance Made Simple for Busy Christians'. Lawrence
and Diane Osborn, whose book *Decisions, Decisions* is a
healthy corrective to such an approach, comment: 'In the
modern era there seems to have been a peculiar emphasis
on the mechanics and techniques of guidance.'[1]

We treat God rather like a computer: we want to
know which buttons to press and in what order. We want
his guidance to unfold in the same way that sheets of
paper appear when we press the 'Print Now' button.
But God is not programmable. While it is his nature to

be consistent we can never predict his responses, because he is beyond our understanding and control. In any case, he delights to do new things in our lives. He will not necessarily respond to our prayers today in the way that he responded yesterday. Neither does he work the same way in two different lives. He knows us as individuals and calls us by name (Isaiah 43:1).

We, on the other hand, prefer to copy others, particularly when they seem successful. Church A grew by adopting strategy X; therefore church B must grow if it adopts the same strategy. Christian A found God's guidance by praying in such-and-such a way; therefore if Christian B prays in the same way she too will discover the secret of God's will for her life. However, while good ideas can be worth borrowing, there is no guarantee that the techniques and methods which work for one church or believer will work for others. If you are looking for the husband or wife of your dreams, a trip to Romania may prove disappointing! It worked for Jo, but it may not work for you.

God is personal and his guidance tends to fit each individual personally. While there are general principles we can follow when we look for his direction in our lives, God does not usually use mechanical techniques. Instead, he prefers to guide us through drawing us into an ever-deepening relationship with himself. I think it was significant that Jo met Jeff only *after* she had let go of the whole business of finding a husband. She had moved on in her relationship with God to a new and deeper level of trust.

For many Christians, guidance consists of figuring out where God wants them at any particular time. 'What job am I to do?' 'What house am I to buy?' 'What person am I to marry?' These things are important, of course and God is deeply interested in all of them. But he is far more interested in the relationship we develop with him. That, after all, will last forever. Furthermore, God is less concerned about giving us guidance and more concerned about being our guide. He does not say, 'Climb the hill, take the first turning on the right, then second left.' He says, 'Come with me.'

Detailed blueprint?

When God says, 'Come with me,' we do not need to hold advance information in our heads. We can be content with knowing just the next step. Have you ever asked for directions and been given a long list of instructions, a list too long to remember? It is hopeless, and you get lost again almost immediately. Some Christians believe that God has a blueprint for every individual in which every last element is mapped out in the minutest detail, point by point. Somehow, the trick is to find the secret that unlocks the plan, or at least as large a section of it as possible. And, at all costs, we must avoid the slightest deviation from God's pre-set purposes. It's a bit like following a treasure trail: each clue has to be located and unearthed before progress to the next can be made.

Certainly God knows every aspect of our lives and is concerned about even the smallest detail – even the hairs on our head are numbered (Matt 10:30) – but does this mean that everything is fixed in advance? Lawrence and Diana Osborn again:[2]

> The blueprint model of guidance effectively turns our pilgrimage into a tightrope walk, a choice of getting it precisely right or disastrously wrong.

The most common biblical picture of God as guide is that of a shepherd. The shepherd is in charge, but the best shepherds know the name of each sheep under their care (John 10:3) and their individual character:

> A shepherd does not completely determine the activity of his sheep. Rather, he leads the flock to good pasture and determines safe limits for its movements. Each sheep is free to move about within those limits. Similarly, we may see much of God's guidance as the setting of safe limits for our freedom.[3]

Dallas Willard goes further:[4]

> The *perfect* will of God may allow, for a particular person, a number of different alternatives. For most people, for example, a number of different choices in selecting a partner (or none at all), various vocations, educational institutions or places of residence may all equally be God's perfect will – none being in themselves 'better' or preferred by God in relation to the ultimate outcome desired by him.

God's 'perfect' will

I am not sure I would entirely agree with Dallas Willard. Sometimes, in the big decisions of life, there *is* only one choice. Married now for six years with two children, I hope Jo still believes that Jeff is the only one God could have had in mind for her as part of his perfect will for her life. But we take Willard's point. In many less significant decisions, there may be no *ideal* choice. Would it really matter if I had bought this house or the identical one next door? Or if I go to London this week or next?

We can get so anxious about uncovering this imagined ideal plan that we miss God's greater desires for our lives. More important than what house we live in, what job we do, or even who we marry, are two things:

- Developing our intimacy with God our Father through Jesus his Son in the power of the Spirit;

- Developing a Christ-like character and a God-honouring lifestyle; what the Bible calls *holiness*.

These two points are brought out clearly in Paul's prayer for the believers at Colosse:

> We ask God to give you a complete understanding of what he wants to do in your lives, and we ask him to make you wise with spiritual wisdom. Then the way you live will always honour and please the Lord, and you will continually do good, kind things for others. All the while, you will learn to know God better and better.
> *(Colossians 1:9–10, NLT)*

A few verses later, Paul expresses the desire that every believer should be 'perfect in Christ' (v 28). In this context, 'perfect' means 'mature' or 'complete'. Over the years, I have noticed that those Christians who adopt a mechanical, push-button approach to guidance, who want every future step neatly plotted out for them, are frequently lacking in maturity. They are like those who want someone to tell them when it is safe to cross the road. This may be appropriate for a four-year-old, but

not a grown-up of forty. As we get to know God better
and desire to please him more, we will find that we have
what Paul calls 'the mind of Christ' (1 Cor 2:16). (In
Part 1, we saw that this was one of the principal means
of God's guidance.)

Although obeying God's will may not get any easier,
knowing it usually does. As our lives are shaped less by
the world and more by the Word, we will more intu-
itively understand God's will for our lives.

The mind of Christ

We can only know someone's mind – someone's
thoughts and feelings – by developing a real relationship
with them. This means spending time with them and
listening to them.

Sometimes one or other church member will come
to me and ask me to pray that God will give them guidance. The first thing I usually do is to enquire about
their spiritual health. It is not uncommon to discover
that the individual concerned has done little to develop
their walk with God, perhaps for some considerable
time. For months, even years, there may have been little
by way of personal Bible reading or prayer. And now,
when there is a difficult decision to be make, they are in
need of God's guidance but do not seem to be getting
any answers. The trouble is, they are out of practice in
hearing God's voice.

God is not like the passer-by in the street whom we
conveniently stop to ask directions. He wants to be a
part of our lives. God is not there to be turned on like a
tap. Major decisions for which we seek God's specific

guidance are, in fact, relatively few and far between.
There is a limited number of times we will move house,
change jobs or get married! But if we only consult God
when we need guidance on the big decisions, we will
find it difficult to discern the mind of Christ or hear his
still small voice speaking at more ordinary times. But if
we make him central to every part of our lives – through
prayer and Bible reading, Christian fellowship, shared
Bible study, corporate prayer and worship and involvement in a ministry or mission, seeking to regulate our
lives by the standards of his Word – then the big decisions will almost take care of themselves. In the words of
the twelfth-century prayer of Richard of Gloucester:

> May we know you more clearly, love you more dearly,
> and follow you more nearly, day by day.

Jo's story

Jo's story, with which this chapter began, has much to
teach us. God often invites us to take the first step of a
journey before he shows us the final step. If we knew
how the journey was going to end before we began,
there would be no need for faith. More likely, if we
could see the end from the beginning, we would probably be too frightened to set out!

When Abraham left Haran for Canaan (Gen 12:1),
he knew only that he was to move from his present loca-
tion. His destination was not revealed until later. It was
only as he was passing through Canaan that God said,
'This is the place' (12:6–7). Would Abraham have set
out if he had known all that lay ahead? The headaches
his nephew Lot would create for him, the difficulty in

conceiving a son and heir, and, later still, that great test of faith when he was asked to sacrifice his son Isaac on the mountain? If I'd been Abraham and had known what was in store, I think I would have stayed at home in Haran. It would have seemed a lot safer.

I was guided to Bible College thinking that I might end up on the mission field. Instead I am in the Baptist ministry. Jo was guided to Romania thinking that that country might be her sphere of Christian service. Instead she is married with a young family and is a valuable member of our church. Was God's guidance deficient or deceptive? Not at all. The problem is not God's guidance, but our perception. We are too eager to see how it will all fall into place. Our common sense sees one way things might work out, but it's as though we are looking through a dirty window. At best, we have only a partial view of God's plan for our lives (1 Cor 13:12). Sometimes God is gracious enough to allow us to glimpse a few steps ahead; mostly he provides just enough light for the step we are on. Too little light and we would be in the dark. Too much light and we would be blinded. Faith is content to take the first step, then let God reveal the next. As an old song I used to sing in my youth group puts it:[5]

> I do not know what lies ahead, the way I cannot see
> Yet one stands near to be my guide; he'll show the way
>   to me:
> I know who holds the future and he'll guide me with
>   his hand,
> With God things don't just happen, everything by him
>   is planned;
> So as I face tomorrow with its problems large and small,
> I'll trust the God of miracles, give to him my all.

Faith and common sense

We are almost at the end of our journey. We have looked at the nature of faith and the character of God, and we have looked at six areas of life that trouble many Christians. The faith by which we are called to live our Christian lives is, in essence, no different from the saving faith which brought us into the Christian life in the first place. It is a faith that rests in a person – the Lord Jesus Christ, who declared himself to be the way, the truth and the life (John 14:6). Faith means putting our trust in what we cannot see (Heb 11:1), in a God who is invisible. But this God we cannot see has revealed himself time and time again in the affairs of human history, and he has done so supremely and definitively in the person of his Son Jesus Christ.

Our faith rests on fact, not feeling. It rests on the historical facts of Jesus' birth, death and bodily resurrection. It looks forward to his promised return and all that will mean in terms of an end to suffering and a final vanquishing of evil. Because faith rests on fact, it is not blind faith but common-sense faith. We can investigate the evidence for ourselves. We can test the guidance we receive. We have God's Word to feed and shape our faith. We can hear God's voice today and we can know the mind of Christ.

But there comes a point beyond which common sense cannot take us. This is because faith is a relationship, not a mechanical exercise. Marriage provides a helpful analogy. When two people are attracted to each other, common sense will tell them whether a permanent relationship is likely to succeed. Do they have enough in common? Do they have compatible temperaments? Do they have similar attitudes to money and to raising children? Do they have coinciding ambitions? But no fulfilled relationship was ever built on common sense alone. There has to be love. And love, as we all know, is not always rational. It goes beyond common sense and sometimes even contradicts it. Love requires trust, just as faith does. Both love and faith must be prepared to take risks.

When a person commits himself to Jesus Christ, he is expressing love for him and exercising faith in him. Common sense will have told him that the Christian life makes more sense than the alternatives. But only faith can seal the relationship.

Trust leads to obedience and faithfulness. Faith is not complete unless it is expressed in obedient action and godly living. Sometimes the call to obedience will come in a moment of crisis, as it was for Peter in the boat. At other times, it will be to a call to faithful service over a lifetime, as it was for Zechariah. Instant obedience in a time of high drama, or a lifetime lived in quiet faithfulness and expectancy: both are an expression of faith. We saw the two come together in Ruth.

Common sense and faith are not enemies. But while common sense is a matter of the mind, faith is a matter of the heart *and* mind – not the heart alone divorced from the mind as some Christians think.

And now, may Christ dwell in your hearts through faith. Being rooted and established in love, may you have power, together with all believers, to grasp how wide and long and high and deep is the love of Christ, and to know this love that is beyond knowing – that you may be filled with all the fullness of God (Eph 3:17–19, my version).

❧ Notes

1. Lawrence & Diana Osborn, *Decisions, Decisions*, IVP, 1996, p 7.

2. Osborn, *Decisions*, p 183.

3. Osborn, *Decisions*, p 24.

4. Dallas Willard, *Hearing God*, p 201.

5. A B Smith & E Clark, *Youth Praise*, CPAS, 1966.

❧ Further reading

Lawrence & Diana Osborn, *Decisions, Decisions*, IVP, 1996.
Bruce Waltke, *Knowing the Will of God*, Kingsway.
Dallas Willard, *Hearing God*, Fount, 1999.

❧ Questions to think about

1. To what extent do you think God has a perfect blueprint worked out for your life? How much freedom do you think he gives you in the choices you have to make?

2. God is more interested in deepening our relationship with him than giving us mechanical, push-button guidance. If you agree, what implications does this have for your priorities as a Christian?

3. Now that you have read this book, what do you think about the relative importance of faith and common sense? Do you need more of one of them, or even both? If so, what steps could you take to make this happen?